"If you're seeking to improve or strengthen the climate and culture of your school, then *Culture by Design: The Discovery Process as a New Way for Schools* is a great resource. *Culture by Design* is not just a book, but an in-depth and detailed guide. Malcolm Gauld provides a blueprint (25 modules) that will assist and support schools in this most necessary endeavor. If we want and expect all students to be academically successful, then we need to make the climate and culture of our schools *the* priority and *Culture by Design* does just that. This is a book that values attitude over aptitude, effort over ability, and character over talent. It is an invaluable resource."

—Jeff Rodman, executive director, New England League of Middle Schools

"Malcolm lays it out when he states quite simply, 'Let us value attitude over aptitude, effort over ability, and character over talent.' He and I have worked alongside each other for years as both fellow heads of school and committed educators. I saw firsthand, and in some cases up close and personally, his focus on getting to the root of education by addressing culture first in our schools. His message is clear, and this book is by a beacon leading the reader forward as well as a toolkit to aid in getting the job done. One can hear Malcolm's voice as you read. And as would be his style, you can also hear his wonderful sense of humor.

This carefully annotated and considered book should be on every head of school's desk. Most importantly, it shouldn't just sit there. It should be an energizing force for school improvement. Malcolm is showing us the path forward."

—James C. Mooney, former head of Vermont Academy, now deputy director of Commission on Independent Schools Accreditation and School Improvement, New England Association of Schools and Colleges

"This is the very rare book that combines rigorous theory with real-world practices—refined to the simplicity beyond complexity from decades of use by master practitioners working with countless teachers, coaches, school leaders, students, and parents. *Culture by Design* provides the perfect vision of *what* culture is and *why* it matters, with concise, flexible, practitioner-friendly materials showing *how* to engage students in meaningful, transformational, real-world practice. More than *knowledge about* character and culture, this resource helps deliver *an experience of* character and culture. It provides everything you need to create the best possible version of your school, which is the foundation for your students unlocking the best possible version of themselves. If your school wants to be (even more) intentional and reflective about culture and character, courage and conscience, confidence and connectedness, everything you want and need can be found in *Culture by Design!*"

—Matt Davidson, Ph.D, president, Excellence with Integrity Institute

Culture by Design

Culture by Design

The Discovery Process as a New Way for Schools

Malcolm Gauld

ROWMAN & LITTLEFIELD
Lanham • Boulder • New York • London

Published by Rowman & Littlefield
An imprint of The Rowman & Littlefield Publishing Group, Inc.
4501 Forbes Boulevard, Suite 200, Lanham, Maryland 20706
www.rowman.com
86-90 Paul Street, London EC2A 4NE, United Kingdom

British Library Cataloguing in Publication Information Available

Library of Congress Cataloging-in-Publication Data

Names: Gauld, Malcolm, 1954– author.
Title: Culture by design: the discovery process as a new way for schools /
    Malcolm Gauld.
Description: Lanham, Maryland: Rowman & Littlefield, 2023. | Includes bibliographical
    references and index. | Summary: "The book is intended as a resource for educators
    seeking to improve student cultures within their schools"—Provided by publisher.
Identifiers: LCCN 2023008641 (print) | LCCN 2023008642 (ebook) | ISBN
    9781475872378 (cloth) | ISBN 9781475872385 (paperback) | ISBN
    9781475872392 (epub)
Subjects: LCSH: School environment—United States. | Classroom environment—United
    States. | School improvement programs—United States.
Classification: LCC LC210.5 .G38 2023 (print) | LCC LC210.5 (ebook) | DDC
    370.15/8—dc23/eng/20230324
LC record available at https://lccn.loc.gov/2023008641
LC ebook record available at https://lccn.loc.gov/2023008642

To Harrison Gauld and Mohamed Jama.
Brothers from different mothers.
My son. My friend.
Forever.

Contents

Preface

"Are you from that place up in Maine?"

Directed at me, the question came from a small-for-his-age fifth grader. I had just arrived at his middle school as a first stop on a tour of a group of public schools in the Harrisburg, Pennsylvania, area. These schools had developed the Discovery Process, a character-based curriculum that embodies aspects of the philosophy and programming long practiced at Hyde School in Bath, Maine.

"Yes, I am," I replied.

My young inquisitor continued, "Are you here to shut down the Discovery Process?"

Feeling like the host on that bygone television show *Kids Say the Darndest Things*, I replied, "No way! I'm just visiting. I heard you folks were doing some great stuff here, and I just wanted to check it out, you know, see it in action for myself."

The fifth grader exclaimed, "Whew! That's good! I used to be afraid to go to school. I was afraid of what was going to happen to me on the bus on the way to school . . . what might happen on the playground . . . and then on the way home. Now I *like* school. The big kids look out for me. It's like a family."

At that point, I turned to the school principal and said, half-joking, "I'm sold. I don't need to see anything else."

Of course, I did see as much as I could and each stop during my tour of these schools confirmed the accuracy of this fifth grader's assessment. I came away from my visit with two questions: 1. Could we develop and scale this thing? 2. How could we not even try?

This book would never have happened, let alone been envisioned, without that visit.

The summer following that visit, a group of educators convened at one of those Pennsylvania schools. Representing public, private, and charter schools, we spent two days exploring two questions:

1. What are the ingredients for the kind of school culture that makes kids feel the way that fifth grader feels?
2. How might we design and build a program that can reflect those ingredients and deliver that culture to any school?

A smaller group met in February of 2019 for a facilitated Design Sprint, a time-constrained, intensive process where participants design and test a prototype product or program in five days. (On day five, in order to secure objective reactions, the group actually pitches the envisioned product to previously unknown potential customers.) The entire first day is spent on one question: What is the problem for which our idea might be an effective solution?

After a full day of heated discussion and debate, we arrived at this consensus on the problem: *School leaders lack a toolkit to help them build and maintain a strong school culture.* Following this Design Sprint, a smaller group of us spent the next three years designing and building that toolkit. All the learning content and training materials would be fully accessible in an online format. We completed it in 2022.

In the midst of our work, everyone's world was rocked by the COVID-19 pandemic. In our case, efforts to launch elements of the program with early adopter schools were thwarted in September of both 2020 and 2021. As of September of 2022, the program is up, running, and fully available to any school.

Why this book? Three reasons. First, it simply seemed that the Discovery Process, with its 134 lessons and nearly ten hours of teacher and school leader training, could use an *off*line companion piece where an overview of the philosophy and mechanics would all be accessible in one place.

Second, while designing and building the Discovery Process, our conversations with countless educators revealed a common administrative pattern within schools. That is, the people in schools with the highest level of decision-making authority were often on the low side of the "tech-savvy" scale. (No judgments! Count the author of this book as one who most definitely falls into this category!) On the other hand, the most tech-savvy educators we spoke with often possessed minimal decision-making authority. When I pointed this out to one superintendent, he agreed, observing that the balance is shifting so fast—partly due to the unexpected demands of COVID-19 on our tech capacities—that this imbalance will not be the case for very long. In the meantime, this book is offered as one way to bridge that gap.

Third, some people, including some very tech-savvy people, simply like books! This book is for them, as well.

Onward,
Malcolm Gauld
Bath, Maine

Acknowledgments

So many people have contributed to this book. Risking the sin of omission, the short list includes:

Pam Hardy, who worked tirelessly with me over two years as we wrote the 134 lessons comprising the inaugural edition of the Discovery Process.

Zach Birnbaum for being my partner in this effort.

The dynamic trio of exemplary Pennsylvania public school educators—Bob Hassinger, David Hatfield, and Jared Shade—who had been fully engaged in the Discovery Process for many years before I ever met them and have been indispensable allies in helping us translate the program into a resource that can be accessed by any teacher at the click of a button.

Lennox K. ("Bim") Black, Steve Carey, Jamie Delaney, Dana and Malcolm McAvity, and J, and Beth Puckett for their belief in and support of this project.

Lucinda Warnick for her expert editorial assistance in reviewing and editing the manuscript.

Mike Therriault for his helpful legal advice and guidance.

Great educators like Sonia Avila, Adam Downing, Sandra Dupree, Barbara High, Matt Kinney, Jen Lebozzo, and Crystal Peltzer, who have contributed their expertise to this effort.

Matt Davidson, a friend and longtime fellow traveler in the character ed lane.

David Dietz, Jacqui Hook, Carrie O'Donnell, and the whole O'Donnell Learn team for dragging me from the familiarity of the analog world to that of digital learning and helping us create this invaluable resource for all teachers and schools.

Tom Koerner and Carlie Wall, and all at Rowman & Littlefield Publishing.

Jim Thornton for his expert advice in helping us maximize the digital customer experience.

Earl Geertgens and Tejas Nerurker for their patient counsel in helping me develop a better understanding of digital learning.

The administration and governing board of Hyde School for their support and for freeing me up to focus on developing the Discovery Process and writing this book.

Laura, Mahalia, Paul, Scout, Liam, and especially, the new guy: P3. What a family!

Introduction

This book is in three parts:

- Part 1: Culture
- Part 2: Discovery
- Part 3: Character

The first two chapters comprising part 1 explore the nature of strong school cultures. What are the ingredients? What are the barriers? What are some of the best practices out there in the educational landscape? What steps might be taken by schools seeking to improve or enhance their culture?

These first two chapters identify, explain, and focus on three crucial components found in nearly any school, business, organization, or community possessing a strong and inspiring culture:

1. a core principle or reason for being
2. a common language reflecting, supporting, and promoting number one
3. a set of practices and traditions reflecting, supporting, and promoting numbers one and two.

Part 2 presents a program—The Discovery Process—as one approach to translating the ideal described in the first two chapters into a reality for any school. Chapters 3 and 4 explore the philosophy, principles, and practices of the program. Chapters 5 and 6 delve more deeply into its nuts and bolts, including a detailed FAQ section.

Part 2 also includes some lessons taken directly from the Discovery Process in order to provide the reader with a clearer picture of the dynamics of the program.

Part 3, encompassed in chapter 7, attempts to answer the question posed in its title: "So, What Is Character?" This question has been circulating . . . and circulating . . . and circulating through the head of the author for nearly half a century. This final chapter shows what he's come up with . . . so far.

Parts of this book fall into different categories: analysis, explanation, memoir, even a bit of promotion. Throughout, the author has attempted to utilize the third-person voice. There are indeed sections where opinions, analysis, and observations are expressed that are based on grounded theory derived from the author's direct experiences. In such cases, the first-person voice is utilized.

PART 1

Culture

Chapter 1

Culture First

One need not listen too hard to hear our schools crying out for reinvention. And anyone who works in schools can tell you that there's nothing like a global pandemic to turn up the volume.

What's the problem? Here's a fifteen-second sound bite: *We care more about what they can do than about who they are . . . and they know it* ("they" = the fifty million students attending our nation's schools).

While COVID-19 has clearly magnified the problem—for example, increasing anxiety and decreasing coping skills—it was here long before we all masked up. Now that we have transferred our KN95s from our faces to our desk drawers for easy access in anticipation of that "just-in-case" scenario, we find that the problem has intensified.

As tempting as it may be to assign blame to the pandemic, the real problem lies with our priorities. And this problem has been percolating for a few generations, having begun before any of today's teachers entered the profession.

What's the solution? Here's another fifteen-second sound bite: *Let us value attitude over aptitude, effort over ability, and character over talent.*

But let's mean it (i.e., posting slogans in the halls while we obsess over getting those test scores up ain't gonna cut it). How do we prioritize these . . . er . . . priorities? By putting culture first in our schools.

We can do this. Hey, we've done it before . . . many times, in fact.

A QUICK HISTORY LESSON

The history teacher in me can't resist a quick lesson on that score:

Thomas Jefferson (1743–1826) started the ball rolling with the (then) radical idea that everybody ought to be educated: "If a nation expects to be ignorant and free, it expects what never was and never will be." While future historians would come to question his perception of the notion of "everybody," he deserves credit for planting the very idea in our heads. He also is one of the few who spoke to both poles of the equality versus excellence debate—that is, how to balance these two objectives—that has raged among educators throughout our history. His founding of the University of Virginia proved to be a timeless example of the latter.

Next came Horace Mann (1796–1859), who echoed Jefferson's call for universal access while pushing for broader aims. A hundred years ago, historian Elwood Cubberly wrote, "No one did more than he to establish in the minds of the American people the conception that education should be universal, non-sectarian, free, and that its aims should be social efficiency, civic virtue, and character, rather than mere learning or the advancement of sectarian ends."[1]

(Note: The world would be a better place if we all lived the wisdom of this Mann quote: "Be ashamed to die until you have won some victory for humanity.")

Born in the year of Mann's death, John Dewey (1859–1952) took a more philosophical, perhaps social engineering position that emphasized an inextricable link between healthy schools and a successful democracy. In his landmark book *Democracy and Education* (1916), he wrote, "A Democracy is more than a form of government; it is primarily a form of associated living, of conjoint communicated experience." For Dewey, the school was the driver of that vision.[2]

Before your eyes glaze over while reading about these three history textbook stalwarts, consider the work of the following people:

- Booker T. Washington (1856–1915) at Tuskegee Institute. Known today as Tuskegee University, it was founded in 1881 as a school committed to training African American teachers.
- Maria Montessori (1870–1952) launched a child-centered philosophy of education that today is practiced across the world in twenty thousand schools (as many as five thousand in the United States).
- Jane Addams (1860–1935), the founder of the field of social work, and her model of reform at Chicago's Hull House.
- W. E. B. DuBois (1868–1963) with his view of "The Talented Tenth" and his help founding the National Association for the Advancement of Colored People.
- Mary McLeod Bethune (1875–1955), founder of schools for African Americans in Daytona, Florida, and beyond, and known in her time as "The First Lady of The Struggle."
- Geoffrey Canada (b. 1952) and his work at the Harlem Children's Zone.

And lest we ignore the efforts of actual students, women like Linda Brown (1943–2018), Dorothy Counts (b. 1942), and Ruby Bridges (b. 1954), who opened the doors to countless others by courageously showing the world what it means to show up . . . no matter what. (Or, to put it another way: whereas most of us grew up worrying about what might happen to us if we skipped school, these young ladies were forced to live in fear of what would happen if they had the audacity to show up!)

Much of the past few decades has been about access to our schools. Thanks to many of these people and others, we have taken great strides in this regard. Speaking personally, as a parent, the educational experiences our son, diagnosed with autism at age three, had in the 1990s and 2000s were vastly superior to what he would have received during my student days in the 1960s and 1970s. (Simply put, we knew "those kids" were in our school, but we not only never interacted with them, somehow those in charge arranged things so that we almost never so much as crossed paths with them. We'd sometimes watch them through the classroom window while they were outside on the playground and we were inside studying our fractions.) As a result, my son was a full-fledged member of his school community during his elementary, middle, and secondary school years. As his father, that was truly heartwarming to behold.

At the outset, let it be known that this book is not about access to our schools. It is not about who is attending our schools. This book is about what happens after they get there.

TEAMS: THEY'RE NOT JUST FOR SPORTS ANYMORE

Ever since the GIs came home after World War II, preparation for college has been the predominant focus of American schools. (To be fair, there have also been significant strides taken in vocational education.) We recently saw this preoccupation veer into a disturbingly unhealthy obsession with the Varsity Blues scandal involving privileged parents scheming for their children's access to some of our most prestigious colleges.

How did we get to that point? How did things go so far off-track?

In the pre-World War II period, schools were largely locally controlled entities that did what parents in their respective geographic regions wanted done. Since then, state and federal guidelines have played much larger roles in everything from compliance with Americans with Disabilities Act mandates to affirmative action guarantees. Mixed in with all the good that these changes have served has been a decrease in local control coupled with a curricular focus that has been tightly sharpened in accordance with the expectations of college admissions departments.

Truth be told, to me, it's fingers on the proverbial chalkboard—Remember chalkboards?—whenever I hear college counselors, administrators, or even parents assuredly pronounce, "But we can't teach x because the selective colleges want to see y." The time has come for secondary-level educators to stop allowing the colleges to dictate our curricular priorities. A more holistic approach to middle and secondary education will ultimately produce better college students, not to mention more fulfilled adults.

Meanwhile, the graveyard of attempted school improvement initiatives continues to grow unabated. Suffice it to say that the idea of educational reform has been an American obsession for a long, long time. As a second-generation educator, my first memory of the "latest thing" goes back to my childhood, when I heard my parents talking about this idea they called the "New Math." (I think my ears perked up because I had already had enough trouble with the old version and shuddered at the assumption that the revised edition would only be harder.)

Since then, it's been quite the revolving door: Values Clarification . . . Progressive Ed . . . Open Classrooms . . . Mainstreaming . . . Self-Pacing . . . Busing . . . Special Ed . . . Back-to-Basics . . . Bilingual . . . the ever-evolving alphabet soup of Learning Differences (ADD, ADHD, ASD, ODD, etc.) . . . Experiential Learning . . . A Nation at Risk . . . Merit Pay . . . No Child Left Behind . . . Anti-Bullying . . . Charters . . . Magnets . . . Multiple Intelligences . . . "Testmania" (my word) . . . SEL . . . E-Learning . . . Distance Learning . . . Home-schooling . . . *Whew!!!*

That's a lot of coming and going. It's time for a time-out. Time to address with uncompromising honesty: Who are we serving? Is it schools and colleges? Or kids and families? Sometimes we get the two priorities mixed up.

Hey, college is great. The goal of gaining admission to a "good school" provided a healthy and productive goal for me as a youngster. And the four years that came as a result—both in and outside the classroom—were profoundly enriching in multiple ways. The pursuit of and the benefits derived from college had a similarly positive impact on my own children. It's hard to perceive studying hard as anything but a good thing. (Striving to learn? . . . I mean, what a concept!) Furthermore, my career has been spent in college preparatory schools, and I believe strongly in the intrinsic value of rigorous college preparatory academics. However . . .

Many schools seem to have ended up in a Catch-22, where they become preoccupied with getting kids to be good at school in order to prepare them for . . . more school. We live in a time when our students, parents, and even the schools themselves sometimes seem unsure of themselves when it comes to drawing the line separating genuine curiosity from credential accumulation. College might well be a much more exciting adventure if our high schools were less conscious of college preparation and more focused on providing a uniquely enriching experience unto themselves.

There's an old school saying that says, "Never kid a kid." Students understand what is going on more than their teachers may realize. Not only have they heard the adage that "the world is run by C students," they also know fully well that some of the biggest "players" currently or recently on the world stage—Gates, Jobs, Dell, Zuckerberg, Turner, Gaga (!)—ultimately turned their backs on the idea of being bound by parental expectations by gaining admission to and enrolling in prestigious universities, only to drop out in order to "grab the gusto" of fame, the big bucks, and those awesome grown-up toys. And look at all those people known the world over by a single name—Beyonce, LeBron, Britney, Rihanna, Whoopi, DiCaprio, Drake, and Jay-Z—who basically didn't go at all! There's no way around it: That's cool!

But that's not the main point here.

When I look back on my own schooling, I have no doubt that my membership on my high school athletic teams was equal in value to my academic classes in terms of preparing me for life, maybe more so. My experiences as an actor in school plays were also powerful, especially the time I forgot my lines as the lead in *Stalag 17* and had to engage in extemporaneous improvisation in the glare of the spotlight.

I also recall the importance of meeting a deadline while writing for the school newspaper, especially given the fact that it came from the student editor, a peer, as opposed to a teacher with a term paper deadline. At the time, I remember thinking, *Our student editor-in-chief is so smooth and sure of himself! Will I be like that when I'm a senior? Will I rally the news staff? Will younger kids listen to me as intently as I am listening to him?* It gave me something to shoot for.

One difference between those extracurricular activities and those college preparatory classes had to do with the fact that in all three of those cases— football, drama, and newspaper—I was a member of a team. We were in it together. We each had a job to do and each of those jobs was important if we were going to succeed—win next Saturday's game, bring the house down and the audience to its feet with applause, have other kids gossiping about the latest edition—as a group. We learned that we needed to both support and challenge each other and had to find the right balance between the two.

Our academic classes, on the other hand, tended to find us all in competition with each other, whether it be for the best rank in class or GPA. It was not uncommon for some teachers to make it clear that there were only so many As that would be given out at the end of the term, so we should "plan accordingly." For sure, I was fortunate to have some great classes where my fellow students and I supported each other. But the team thing was never as powerful as it was in that extracurricular realm.

What if learning, school itself, could occur in a team format? What if we set time aside for kids to support, challenge, and inspire the best out of each other? It's not a complicated change. Any school can do it. This book explores that goal and includes ways that some schools have taken that very step.

IF TEAMS ARE THE SOLUTION, WHAT'S THE PROBLEM?

The problem is on two levels: the seen and the unseen. Let's start with "The Seen" problems.

The Seen. Bullying and the Shortcomings of Thinking: *Cure.*

Like a fire alarm, the seen problems are hard to miss or ignore. What's more, the COVID-19 pandemic has magnified them. Consider bullying. As of this writing, all fifty of the United States have now passed some form of anti-bullying legislation. Stop for a moment and think about that. I mean, all fifty?!

Remember those old "How-a-Bill-Becomes-a-Law" diagrams that appeared in textbooks of old? Think about how s-l-o-o-o-o-w of a process that is. Then think about what would have to be going on in our schools, our families, and our communities to compel all those legislators to come together to engage in the endless give and take necessary to turn a bill, any bill, into a law. Then think about the fact that all fifty of our states have been sufficiently moved to engage in that very arduous process.

One need not look hard for data explaining this change in priorities. During the past five years:

- The National Center for Education Statistics shows that one in five public school students report being bullied. (Incidents among girls approach one in four.) [3]
- What's more, 41 percent of those who have been bullied live in fear of it happening again.
- The Centers for Disease Control and Prevention (CDC) report that as many as 30 percent of all middle school students have experienced cyber-bullying.[4]
- A 2017 GLSEN National School Climate Survey shows that 60 percent of America's LGBTQ students feel unsafe in school due to their sexual orientation.[5]

A full two years before COVID-19 changed our world, a group of colleagues and I began working on a project we loosely called "a school culture improvement program." Not only has the pandemic magnified these statistics, but any teacher today will also tell you it has given rise to a heightened sense of anxiety among students, teachers, and parents.

For example, in a 2022 survey of 7,705 high school students, the CDC found that 44 percent of these students described persistent feelings of sadness or hopelessness that prevented them from participating in normal activities. What's more, 9 percent admitted to having attempted suicide. These statistics boil down to an unmistakable conclusion: Now, more than ever, school culture matters.[6]

Schools simply cannot serve as providers of enriching, to say nothing of transformative, experiences if the students within must spend any time feeling physically threatened, publicly humiliated, or virtually maligned. At the same time, it is not enough for a school to be a place where kids feel safe. (Talk about a low bar!) School must be a place where they feel encouraged, indeed inspired, to test their abilities, hopes, and dreams.

The Unseen. Missed Inspiration Resulting from Not Thinking: *Prevention and Enhancement.*

Anyone leading a school thinks a lot about culture, especially bad culture. That's because strong culture has a way of being both undetected and unappreciated until it turns, well, bad. Bad would be defined as an increase in bullying, vaping, insubordination, or various other toxicities. *Or* as a notable decrease in academic performance in the classroom or sportsmanship on the playing field. Then we start thinking more about culture, what is going wrong, and how to put things back on track. (Although we often don't consider the possibility that the "back on track" we've idealized is not as good in practice.)

In a nutshell, when it comes to culture, schools tend to think *cure* as opposed to *prevention* or *enhancement*. That order of prioritization has a way of leading to a myopic focus on symptoms, sometimes leaving the causes to multiply in intensity.

A recent University of California study evaluated and ranked fifty-three anti-bullying programs. First off, the very fact that there are at least fifty-three anti-bullying programs in the United States—the study did not stipulate how many other programs it simply chose not to evaluate—puts an exclamation point on the problem. Second, it also recalls a long-ago episode of *I Love Lucy,* where Ricky enters the house—"Lucy! I'm home!"—only to find her searching the carpet, crawling on all fours. When she explains that she is searching for a lost earring, Ricky helpfully inquires, "You lost it in the living room?" To which Lucy responds, "No, I lost it in the bedroom, but the light is so much better here."

Many contemporary anti-bullying programs fall into a "make it absent" default zone, one heavy on identifying and penalizing behavioral violations.

(Some even take a scorched-earth approach, where even teasing—a normal part of adolescence—is classified as bullying.) This mindset reflects the mathematician's maxim of "necessary but not sufficient." Even if you manage to make bullying absent, it does not necessarily follow that an inspiring *esprit de corps* will be present. Rather than start with what to do about bullying, why not ask the more holistic question: *What to do about inspiration?*

Enroll in any undergraduate or graduate course in education and it will not be long before you will consider and debate a recurring timeless question: *Is society a reflection of our schools, or are our schools a reflection of society?* While few of these discussions will ever evolve to a point of a shared consensus, everyone will likely agree that schools and society inform each other constantly in perhaps a back-and-forth relationship.

Professor Steven Rockefeller addresses this factor in his powerful 2022 book *Spiritual Democracy and Our Schools: Renewing the American Spirit with Education for the Whole Child*. He observes, "Under the impact of polarization, pandemic, and economic hardship, the mood of the country tends to be anxious, angry, and pessimistic."

Rockefeller explains that the list of causes fueling this mood is long, ranging from the unprecedented partisan bitterness in our national politics, as manifested in the January 6 assault on the US Capitol, to the aftermath of the murder of George Floyd, which gave dramatic rise to the Black Lives Matter movement to alarming rates of drug and alcohol abuse among our young and even suicide attempts among teenagers.

After describing many of our problems and issues as a society, he argues:

> *Any serious endeavor to overcome this multi-dimensional crisis gripping the nation will have to find ways to address the deeper source of the condition in which the American people find themselves. The underlying problem is the erosion and weakening of America's moral and spiritual foundations, reflecting estrangement from our better selves and one another and the larger community of life on Earth. So many of the country's leaders and ordinary citizens have lost faith in a shared set of core American values that are considered sacred, transcend all political and social differences, and provide a unifying sense of national identity and common purpose. As a number of leaders have asserted, America is a nation in search of its soul. There is an urgent need for a rediscovery of ideas and values that can once again serve as an inspiring, healing, and unifying force.[7]*

If Professor Rockefeller is right—Heck, even if he is half right!—there is no way that our schools, and more specifically the culture within our schools would not be deeply affected by these societal changes. Rather than wait around for the national culture to change for the better, perhaps our schools can lead the way for a national culture turnaround and a brighter future for all.

In order to make the changes necessary for schools to take this leadership role in society, a change of priorities is essential. In a 2022 *International Journal of Educational Research* article ("Awakened Schools: The Burning Imperative of Pedagogical Relational Culture"), authors Amy Chapman and Lisa Miller state:

> *The major societal failings in the United States are, at their root, a failure of the focus and method of education. American schools focus almost exclusively on subject matter and narrow academic skills, which has become endemic to civic education as well. This has led to the disintegration of the strategic head, knowing heart, and purposeful hands: in effect, students are knowers of content who are disconnected from action and connection with fellow people and nature. Schools are attending to specifics of what students know, but are largely disregarding who students become or what they do in the lived world with new knowledge.[8]*

Chapman and Miller continue:

> *This focus only on the academic preparation of students has resulted in too many adults who know content but who have difficulty translating this learning into engaged relational civic perspective taking. We see this in the civic sphere, locally and nationally, in the interactions people have with the people they meet every day. The Pew Center for Research found that a majority of Americans try to avoid those with whom they deeply disagree and that a supermajority of both Republicans and Democrats are afraid of members of the other party. If people in the United States cannot even interact with each other without avoidance and fear, we have clearly moved away from the active, morally and spiritually informed civic participation envisioned by Mann and Dewey.*

In the second half of this book, we will explore the work that a small cohort of schools have done in developing the Discovery Process as a school culture enhancement program for their students and teachers. For sure, the educators leading these schools were concerned about bullying and all the other glaring culture issues facing contemporary schools. However, it is perhaps instructive to examine the motivations they had that compelled them to consider a program designed to enhance school culture.

First, their motivations were not primarily problem oriented. Rather than ask, *How do we stop these kids from bullying?* they asked, *How do we inspire these kids?*

Bob Hassinger is a retired former principal and superintendent of schools in Halifax, Pennsylvania. He established the very first Discovery Process program as a first-time principal in 1997 at Halifax Middle School. He explains what motivated him to try something (anything) new.

Every school has a culture. In most schools that culture is created by default. What happens in the bus or in the hallways when the teachers aren't looking is not created by design. It's just what happens. In our case, we were seeing students from good families who were not making good decisions because they were finding themselves up against a less-than-productive peer group culture that was very powerful. Simply put, at our school, we decided that the culture we had was not working for us. So, we wanted to design a culture that would work with what supportive parents wanted for their children and actually support that culture within the school.

Dr. David Hatfield, the current superintendent of schools in Halifax, observes:

We thought it was important to build connections with our students and reach them at a deeper level. For us, it wasn't about trying to supplant parents, or churches, or organizations in our community in teaching character. It was really about reinforcing what parents and organizations in the community were already trying to impart to the kids.

We had kids that were living in two separate worlds, really. They had a school persona lots of times, and they had an outside-of-school persona. And we really wanted to marry those two things together, touch kids genuinely and allow them to grow and develop socially and emotionally.

Sometimes, the things that educators value—academics and good behavior— were not seen as cool things. So, we really needed to work on our school culture to make sure that the educators and the students shared the same set of values and expectations.

To be sure, both Hassinger and Hatfield were concerned about bullying and they were anything but strangers to the range of attitudinal and behavioral issues facing schools. However, their primary motivations to consider some different approaches were more about inspiration than problem-solving.

Jared Shade, superintendent of schools at the neighboring Upper Dauphin (Pennsylvania) Area School District, put it this way:

I'll never forget when one parent said to me, "If nothing else, I want my child to be kind and courteous and respectful, and to be known for that." That's what we want as a community. The philosophy is to create a culture where students feel safe to learn and one that is equitable for all students. Too often, when we enter schools, the roof and the walls are on the school but the foundation is not underneath that floor and walls. So, in order to maintain the integrity of the roof and walls, we need a strong foundation. And the Discovery Process helps us do that.

Upper Dauphin master teacher Adam Downing concurs:

The philosophy behind the Discovery Process is that academics provide only one part of educating the whole child. When a student comes here to school, obviously they're here to learn about the things that are in their content classes: math, science, reading, etc. Discovery helps us look at the other side of the community. It helps students develop personally and teaches them how to become a member of a community.

He also adds a contemporary teacher's perspective to the comments made by these three superintendents.

We're experiencing more responsibilities as educators than we ever have before. We're not just teachers. We're counselors. We are stand-in parents from time to time. Sometimes it can even feel that we're stand-in doctors. In some cases, we're security, we're soldiers, and we're all these things we never really signed up to be.

Downing is representative of the teachers are highly committed to doing whatever it takes to help students. His statement about the increase in responsibilities facing teachers today is neither cynical nor a call for a return to the so-called good old days. It is simply a statement of fact: When educational conditions change, teachers and school leaders also need to change.

He continues,

I've been a part of other canned character ed or anti-bullying programs. They usually involve big, thick binders, with pages and pages of paper and lots of worksheets. They feel like something you have to do rather than want to do. It feels hollow to me, and when it feels hollow to me, the kids see right through it. They always know what's really going on.

As Jared Shade states, "There needs to be a sense of urgency for creating this culture. We're seeing school shootings, school violence. There needs to be a sense of urgency. Not to buy a product. Not to buy a program, but to change our culture."

So, let's get to it!

When we launched our Discovery Process initiative in 2018, we had candid discussions with scores of educators about their own school culture issues or problems. This quickly led us to a top ten list:

1. Bullying, both cyber and physical
2. Fear and anxiety
3. Disruptive behavior

4. Indifference toward classes or activities
5. Lack of trust and teamwork between school and home
6. Obsession with electronics: cell phones, social media, gaming
7. Students "slipping through the cracks"
8. Multicultural and/or racial issues
9. Sex and gender issues
10. Substance abuse

What we did not know in 2018 was that the veritable COVID-19 tsunami lying in wait would soon magnify these issues and add new ones.

So, our initial motivation to get into this social emotional learning/character education/school culture space came from a belief that our schools would be vastly better places of learning and preparation for life if they could transition to a priority of putting culture first. (Note: As a forty-five-year educator in the character ed lane, the author has always believed this.) Then, suffice it to say that the COVID-19 pandemic didn't exactly do anything to convince us otherwise. Beyond our initial motivations and the pandemic, there is also the matter of dealing with teenagers . . . in any era! As kids approach the middle school years, they inevitably face a conflict between what is right versus what is cool. Add a counterproductive school culture to this dilemma (in the midst of a worldwide pandemic), and the prospects for transformative adolescent development are seriously threatened.

SOME RANDOM INGREDIENTS FOR
STRONG SCHOOL CULTURES

While this book was in its early stages, a number of dedicated and respected educators were approached and asked to identify some of the ingredients for ensuring a strong school culture. Here are some of the answers received:

Common Language

"Our school culture benefits from a **collection of words and principles** that truly guide what we're doing, how we live our lives, how we approach each other and situations. We share a vision that serves as a glue that helps us move each other forward."—Dr. Sandra Dupree, *executive director, Hyde Public Charter School, Brooklyn, New York*

"Having a **common language** puts every student and every adult on the same playing field. As teachers, it allows us to bridge gaps with students that we may not know well or students with whom we don't typically interact."—Adam Downing, *social studies teacher, Upper Dauphin (Pennsylvania) Middle School*

Student to Student

"Our culture is at its strongest when kids are not only responsible for themselves and the choices they make, but when they have a part in encouraging others to make good choices as well and also to contribute. Nobody is a bystander. We all have a part to play in helping our classmates to be and do better."—Dr. David Hatfield, *superintendent of schools, Halifax, Pennsylvania*

Teamwork and the No Blame Game

"Student failure is treated as **everyone's problem**, and adults don't blame each other, but work together. Parents don't blame the teacher and vice versa."—Craig Cunningham, PhD, *professor of education*

"**School-wide jobs** (a component of the Discovery Process) inspire kids to take **ownership** of the school. I'll never forget a custodian who came up to me when I was a young principal and said, 'Boy, you must be a real disciplinarian who scares the kids because graffiti and litter in the halls have just disappeared.' I replied, 'It's not because I'm a disciplinarian. It's because these kids are owning the school as theirs.'"—Jared Shade, *superintendent of schools, Upper Dauphin, Pennsylvania*

An Effective Advisory Program

"There are a lot of benefits to the school culture that come from an effective advisory program. First, every student is known well by at least one adult in the school who can be an advocate and sometimes a nudge for the student. Second, the student is part of a group of peers, hopefully that stays together over four years of high school, who don't necessarily start as friends, but over time come to appreciate and care for each other. It is important that the advisory does things together that pull them tighter and not just manufactured team-building activities. . . . An effective advisory program means that students know their advisory is the go-to place for supporting one another. Another important role for advisory is to have a place to talk about important culture issues in the school within a trusted group. An interesting outcome on the professional culture is that every adult in the school becomes really familiar, through the student perspective, of the four-year experience in the school, allowing for the appreciation of the work of their colleagues across all subject areas and grade levels."—Ted Hall, *former senior associate at*

Great Schools Partnership, Inc., Portland, Maine (retired); former principal,
Yarmouth (Maine) High School

Expectations, Leadership, Awareness, and Ethos

"I visited a great classroom culture yesterday at a small public elementary school in rural Maine. I witnessed **high expectations**. A **mutual respect** between teacher and student. Some **fun and levity** in the learning process. And, importantly, a **sense of purpose** to it all. Students were clearly engaging their time and effort in the learning process because they saw the reason and the benefit to them (e.g., aspirations)."—Bob Stuart, *executive director, Maine College Circle, Yarmouth, Maine*

"**Leadership matters**! Leaders must model what they want to see from students, staff, and communities."—Chris Toy, *former public school principal (Maine)*

"It comes down to **social and emotional awareness** and the students' feel the school asking 'Who are you?' and not just 'What are you capable of doing?'"—Jen Lobozzo, *Spanish teacher, Hyde School, Bath, Maine*

Anyone who has taught for any length of time would likely agree with all of the observations made by these educators. I know I do. The question, then, becomes one of structure and prioritization. We must have a vision of a good culture before we can hope to attain it. It can also help to distinguish between culture and climate.

CULTURE VS. CLIMATE

So, if bad culture is easy to spot, what does good culture look like? What are its ingredients?

If you are a school leader or superintendent, you have many hats to wear. The short list of your oversight responsibilities would include budgets, hiring, facilities, scheduling, athletics, dining, staff, code compliance, curriculum, and security. The only thing more daunting than that list would probably be the long list! However, amid all the duties and responsibilities that go with either of those lists, make sure you take the time to ask yourself, "At this moment, how would I rate the quality of our school culture?" You can delegate some of this responsibility, but only you can truly own it.

Speaking personally, one way that I own it is with a simple monthly ritual borrowed from the work of Jeff Beedy of Sports PLUS and Eric Schaps of the Developmental Studies Center, two great character educators, both recently deceased. At the beginning of each month, I jot down the following notes at

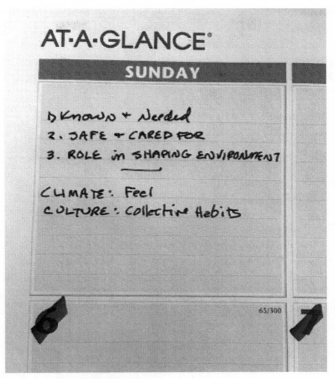

Figure 1.1   Note on Author's Desk Calendar
Malcolm Gauld

the top of my desktop calendar (Fig. 1.1). Items 1–3 refer to the way I want students at our school to feel each and every day:

1. *Known and Needed:* Their names are known, and they have a sense that the school would not be the same (or as good) without them. No one is invisible. No one slips through the cracks.
2. *Safe and Cared For:* Not only do the students believe that they are safe and cared for, but the faculty also believe and ensure it. As one Discovery Process superintendent said to me, "Our goal is for each and every student in our school to have at least one adult advocate."
3. *Role in Shaping Environment:* The students are not mere cogs in the machine. They feel as though they possess some capability to influence the quality of daily school life. And this feeling is valid.

This simple monthly act can serve as a helpful reminder of what's truly important, especially when one is caught up in the daily routine demanded by the aforementioned short or long lists of administrative issues.

As important as those three points on the desk calendar may be, they have to do with school climate as opposed to culture. That brings us to the second set of desktop calendar jottings:

Climate: Feel

Culture: Collective Habits

The words "climate" and "culture" are often thrown around interchangeably in school conversations. Although the two are mutually supportive, they mean two different things.

Climate involves how people—students, teachers, janitors, visiting athletic teams, administrators, spectators in the football stands, local merchants, alumni, etc.—feel about what is (and perhaps what is not) happening at school.

Culture involves actual behaviors, habits, traditions, and practices.

To explain, it is common for schools to distribute surveys that ask questions like:

- Do you feel safe in the school building?
- Do you have an adult at school that you feel you can talk to about your hopes or fears?
- Does bullying happen at your school?
- Do new students feel welcomed at school?
- Do you feel encouraged to try new extracurricular activities?

Those questions are designed to get a read on how the students feel about the social atmosphere at school. They can help administrators understand and assess the school's climate. To be sure, the responses to those questions are not irrelevant to the school's culture. Specifically, if the answers to those five questions are No, No, Yes, No, and No, then it is reasonable to assume that such a school would have significant problems with both climate and culture. The two are not only related, but they are also intertwined.

Turning to culture, the focus is on actual behaviors. What are the patterns of behavior that make students feel as they do about the climate? How can we, as teachers, provide values-forming lessons and challenges that will help them explore their own attitudes about both climate and culture? Perhaps it will be useful to examine three lessons from the Discovery Process specifically designed to facilitate that exploration.

1. Leave It Better Than You Found It, from the *Caring* Module

Here is the explanation from the Discovery Process lesson:

A great athletic program has talented athletes and a whole community of play-ers, coaches, and fans who tend to show a lot of class in the way they conduct themselves. Here is a true story about a high school basketball program—we'll call the school Elmhurst—where everyone does just that. Each February, the Elmhurst basketball team and fans descend upon the state's largest athletic center for the state basketball tournament. One year as fans were filing out of the arena after a game, a janitor pulled an Elmhurst faculty member aside and said, "I probably shouldn't say this, but me and my guys always cheer for Elmhurst at this thing. Not only do we love watching your players and your fans, we also know that we don't need to clean up after the Elmhurst folks. Fact is, my guys fight over who gets the job of cleaning up the Elmhurst section after you guys leave."

Years ago, Elmhurst established the ethic of "Leave It Better Than You Found It." This is a step beyond "Pick Up after Yourself." Once you step up to the higher standard, it is no longer acceptable to say, "I didn't make that mess, so I don't have to clean it up." It all started decades ago during "away" athletic events when our coaches would get after the kids to make sure that they didn't leave paper cups and athletic tape on the ground or floor. This evolved into, "Let's be sure to clean up our area."

Before long, it reached a point where some of teams would clean up their locker room no matter how clean it was when they arrived. This eventually became a trademark of Elmhurst athletic teams. Ultimately, the ethic spread beyond sports and into classrooms, meeting spaces, dining areas, buses, side-walks, even movie theaters. It's not rocket science. In fact, anyone can do it!

"Leave It Better Than You Found It" is a culture "thing." While it contributes to and reflects climate, it differs in a very concrete way: It is easy to check and see if it is actually happening. All that a coach has to do is take a walk through the locker room after the last player leaves and see for themselves how clean it is. A quick look will tell them if the collective habit is real or not.

2. Give'em Seven, from the *Best Possible Me/Us* Module

In honor of friendliness, Discovery Process schools are big on encouraging students and teachers to go out of their way to introduce themselves to cam-pus newcomers. We like to say, "Give'em Seven: five fingers and two eyes." (We actually practice doing that!) So, in terms of the climate/culture dynamic, people typically characterize Discovery Process schools as friendly places. That's climate. (And, again, that's a good thing!) When we see kids introduc-ing themselves to others and sometimes making jokes about the "Give'em

Seven" thing, we take that as a sign that the culture, at least the friendliness aspect of it, is kicking in.

So when you come to campus and you find kids and teachers "giving you seven," you might conclude that the friendliness feature of the culture is in good working order. If not, well, let us know! (Any school that is serious about culture knows that an ongoing commitment to continuous improvement is a given.)

3. The One Thing, from the *Commitment* Module

The One Thing is short for "The One Thing I Will Do Each Day, Not Try to Do." Here is the explanation from the Discovery Process lesson:

Most of us want to improve the quality of our lives, but too often we are willing to make only vague commitments such as: "OK, I guess I'll work harder on my homework." Although we may be sincere when we make these commitments, competing interests or obligations often then get in the way. All too often we become overwhelmed with factors that are out of our control and we make excuses. For example:

- *"The teacher has it in for me."*
- *"I've created a bad reputation for myself."*
- *"I've fallen too far behind."*
- *"I just don't get this stuff!"*

So, you must ask yourself, "Can I control whether or not Mr. XYZ likes me?" (Correct answer: No.) Then ask, "Can I control whether I show interest in his class by raising my hand to speak at least once per class period?" (Correct answer: Yes.) Now you have the perfect framing for a personal goal that can become your "One Thing," something you will do each day, not try to do.

Here's a story about how the One Thing got started by a high school soccer coach: After a few games, the coach analyzed the team's play and statistics and called a team meeting. To a strong-footed girl who tended to miss the net, the coach said, "Twenty shots on net before every practice, that's your One Thing." She asked another player to do fifteen head balls before practice. She asked another to do a dozen corner kicks. As the players began to embrace the system, it was common for them to discuss the concept routinely at team meetings. For example, one player would say, "I've been messing up a lot of scoring chances lately, so I'm thinking of switching my One Thing to twenty break-aways before practice." Another might suggest to a teammate, "Sally, maybe you should switch your One Thing to fifteen throw-ins." When others know your One Thing, they can help keep you on track.

So, returning to our climate/culture dynamic, students and teachers might feel that athletes at their school try hard. That's climate. However, when you hear the words "one thing" peppered in those jovial hallway conversations that happen in all schools, that's culture.

REGULAR (PULSE) CHECKUPS

For teachers and school leaders, no job is more important than that of ensuring a safe, enriching, and inspiring school culture. To accomplish this, the ability to make a quick assessment of that quality is critical. Some Discovery Process schools call it "checking the pulse." Although the modules and lessons of the Discovery Process have been designed to serve as tools for teachers to use in support of their students, some of them can be utilized by faculty and administrators for purposes of "pulse checking."

For example, chapter 5 of this book presents a description of each module and lesson comprising the Discovery Process. Module 2—*The Debrief*—teaches students how to conduct a "Debrief" following an activity or in response to an issue impacting the students or their community. That same concept can be utilized by teachers and administrators during a faculty meeting as a culture assessment tool. Similarly, the "Stop/Start/Continue" exercise in the *Clear the Decks* module can be utilized multiple times during a school year. It asks any group—a homeroom, an athletic team, a school club, a faculty, a school board, etc.—to consider three simple questions:

1. What do we need to stop doing?
2. What do we need to start doing?
3. What do we need to continue doing?

Once it becomes internalized in a school culture, it can become common for a teacher or administrator to pipe up at a meeting with, "Maybe it's time for a 'Stop, Start, and Continue.'" It's quick, easy, and can often give us a useful read on how our culture is doing.

Utilizing the modules and lessons in our daily work life at school can have another hidden benefit: It shows the students that the concepts and lessons of the Discovery Process are not just something they are required to do. We, the adults, also do them. And when we do that, we model what we are teaching them.

OK, if we know what culture is and how it compares and contrasts with climate, then how do we build culture? That is the subject of the next chapter.

A PROPOSED READER MINDSET

Before transitioning to a more "how-to" emphasis, I'd like to propose a particular mindset or frame of reference for the reader. Consider a routine I have used for decades with assembled groups of teenagers across the country.

First, I ask for a show of hands in response to a simple question: "How many of you have ever been told that you are a bright kid who doesn't apply themselves?" Amid chuckles, most hands are invariably raised.

Then, I might ask, "How many of you have ever been told, 'You are a hard worker despite the fact that you are not all that bright'?" While the room fills with what I might term confused laughter, no hands go up.

The point? Adult assessments of middle and high school student scholastic performance nearly always begin with the brightness factor. Once that is established, the consideration of effort commences. It has always reminded me of the tether ball station on a playground. The stationary pole represents the level of brightness while the ball spinning around on the rope represents effort. New programs, initiatives, and curricular emphases may come and go, but our national preoccupation with brightness, intelligence, and general academic ability is deeply engrained in our consciousness as the unalterable constant.

Returning to my student assembly, I go on to explain that I frequently heard the "You're a bright kid, but . . . " line as a kid, especially during numerous student–parent–teacher conferences during my middle school years. I pretty much tuned them out, inwardly dismissing such verbiage as polite "adult-speak," utilized to keep my parents from getting too worked up. (Privately, I cynically wondered, *If you thought I was not bright, would you say that in this conference?*)

Years later, my wife, Laura, and I co-authored a parenting book titled *The Biggest Job We'll Ever Have,* and we addressed this matter in a section subtitled "'You're a Bright Kid Who Doesn't Apply Himself' and Other Hollow Phrases."

To quote from that book:

As teachers and parents ourselves, we might consider a simple choice: Either we believe that attitude is more important than aptitude or we believe that aptitude is more important than attitude.

Our experience has been that most people will profess to believe that attitude is the more important of the two. ("Honey, I don't care about the grade as long as you try your hardest.") Yet many of today's schools and families actually operate as though they value aptitude more than attitude, whether they intend to or not. We frequently ask high school students if they know any students at their schools who do very little academic work and yet consistently make the honor roll. Not only do they acknowledge that this practice is common, the way they acknowledge it is more than a bit disheartening: "Sure, that's the way it's always been. Some kids just 'have it' and school rewards them." Many point admiringly to the student who is able to get the A with next to no effort.

As educators and parents, we have come to believe that the valuation of aptitude over attitude is crippling our schools and our families in ways we don't even realize. The bright kids know they don't really need to work hard, and the average to below-average ones don't believe their efforts will be rewarded in any significant way. . . . How can we possibly believe that we can inspire genuine learning and character development in a system where our students do not believe that their best efforts will be respected?[9]

So, when thinking about school culture and how to improve it, try looking at your school's objectives, practices, and priorities through a fresh set of eyes. How about putting effort first?

What would things look like if we placed our highest value on attitude, effort, and character?

Carole Dweck, in her groundbreaking book *Mindset—The New Psychology of Success*, refers to what she calls a "fixed" versus a "growth" mindset.

- The Fixed Mindset perceives intelligence as static. It places a premium on looking smart, which, in turn, can lead one to avoid challenges (for fear of looking "un-smart"), devalue effort, ignore or become defensive regarding feedback from others, and feel threatened by or envious of the success of others. As a result, those with a fixed mindset are prone to plateau early or fall short of their potential.
- The Growth Mindset perceives intelligence as a quality than can be developed. It embodies a desire to learn and a tendency to embrace new and unfamiliar challenges. Those with a Growth Mindset tend to persist in the face of setbacks, perceive effort as the key ingredient for mastery, and both value and learn from criticism. Not only are they not threatened by the success of others, but they are also inspired by it as they continue on their journey to ongoing new levels of personal growth and achievement.[10]

So rather than perceiving our students through the lens of how bright they may be and then determining how hard they try in relationship to that level of "brightness," why not look at it the other way around? Start with perceiving how hard they try while engaged in their schoolwork and their extracurricular activities. If your school has a core belief, a motto, or a shared common language, consider the extent to which the student tries to embody those qualities. Then, and only then, move your thinking to how bright the student may happen to be.

Aptitude, ability, and talent are all developable, but that development sometimes takes a very long time to materialize. The great thing about a focus on attitude, effort, and character is that we humans possess the capability to change all three instantaneously. Similarly, any school that wants to change or improve its culture cannot expect to do so overnight. However, the commitment to making that change can start right away.

NOTES

1. Cubberly, Elwood, *Public Education in the United States* (Boston: Houghton Mifflin, 1919).

2. Dewey, John, *Democracy and Education* (Stuttgart: Macmillan, 1916).

3. National Center for Education Statistics, "Bullying at School and Electronic Bullying," https://nces.ed.gov/programs/coe/indicator/a10.

4. Centers for Disease Control and Prevention, "#StopBullying," https://www.cdc.gov/injury/features/stop-bullying/index.html.

5. GLSEN, "The 2017 National School Climate Survey," https://www.glsen.org/research/2017-national-school-climate-survey.

6. Centers for Disease Control and Prevention, https://www.cdc.gov/.

7. Rockefeller, Steven C., *Spiritual Democracy and Our Schools: Renewing the American Spirit with Education for the Whole Child* (London: Clearview Publishing, 2022).

8. Chapman, Amy, and Lisa Miller, "Awakened Schools: The Burning Imperative of Pedagogical Relational Culture," *International Journal of Educational Research* 116 (2022): 102089.

9. Gauld, Laura, and Malcolm Gauld, *The Biggest Job We'll Ever Have* (New York: Scribner, 2002).

10. Dweck, Carol, *The Growth Mindset: The New Psychology of Success* (New York: Random House, 2006).

Chapter 2

Building Good Culture:
Three Components

Throughout the process of creating and building the Discovery Process, the topic of culture was ever-present. Who has it? How do you get it? How do you keep it? While the process seems to be unique to every school or setting, every strong culture we observed seemed to reflect an interplay involving three components:

1. a **core principle** permeating the entity or a deeply shared reason for existence
2. a **common language** reflecting that core principle or reason for existence
3. a set of **practices or traditions** supporting numbers one and two

This chapter explores all three.

MISSION, VISION, AND PLAN—
THE BUS DRIVER ANALOGY

While these three culture-building components all serve the same end—to deliver and maintain an inspiring culture—they each have distinct roles in that deliverance. Before exploring them separately here, consider an analogy of a bus driver with a mission, a vision, and a plan.

Let's assume that the bus driver's mission is to provide safe, reliable, affordable, and comfortable transportation throughout the continental United States. (Relating this to school culture, consider the mission as akin to a school's core principle or reason for existence.)

Next, the bus driver's vision is to drive from New York City to Los Angeles in three days. (Vision is akin to common language.)

Finally, the bus driver's plan is to take a northerly route on I-70 and I-80. (Plan is akin to practices and traditions.)

Once the journey begins, the bus driver can encounter unforeseen problems (e.g., major construction on I-80 or tornadoes forecasted for I-70) that might cause him to revise his plan. Perhaps the riders on the bus all take a vote and decide that they want to take a detour to Yellowstone National Park for a day.

This turn of events might well cause the bus driver to consider the wishes of his passengers and add an extra day: "OK, people, our new vision is to travel from New York to Los Angeles in four days instead of three." This decision to change the vision carries more ramifications than might occur as a result of changing the plan (i.e., the driving routes). There will likely be anger from those passengers who voted against the trip to Yellowstone and might have scheduled appointments to keep in Los Angeles.

That brings us back to mission. It is possible that the bus company could unexpectedly triple the cost of the bus fare, causing the bus driver to tell the passengers to pay up or get off. (So much for affordability.) The bus company might also decide to take out the bathroom at the rear of the bus and replace it with two more rows of seats. (There goes comfort.)

The point? If we translate the bus driver analogy to the work of a school in developing and/or maintaining a strong culture, the school's practices, like the bus driver's plan, are reasonably adaptable and changeable. The school's common language can change, but perhaps not as easily as its practices. The school's mission borders on the sacred. Although it is not impervious to change—and schools can change their mission for some good reasons—it is not all that far from it. Otherwise, it will not be taken seriously by the school community that has embraced it. In turn, a mission not taken seriously can result in watered down common language, practices, and traditions.

Let's explore each of these three factors in more detail.

1. Core Principle *or* Reason for Existence

As an educator writing a book for educators, perhaps it makes sense for me to begin with the most famous core principle from our field (Fig. 2.1).

Ve Ri Tas is Latin for truth.

From the Harvard University (founded in 1636) website:

> *Veritas eventually was discovered in old college records by Harvard President Josiah Quincy III, and re-emerged in 1836 when it appeared on a banner celebrating the College's 200th anniversary. The word briefly lived on in the Harvard seal from 1843 to 1847, when it was booted off in favor of Christo et Ecclesiae, or "For Christ in the Church."*

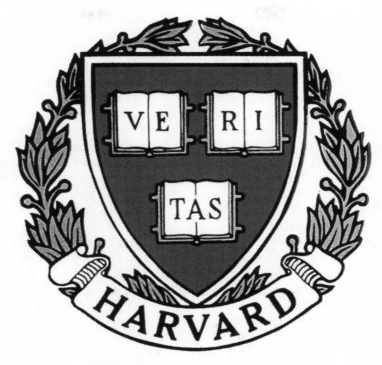

Figure 2.1 Harvard University Crest
Wikipedia

In time, Veritas would become the one word most closely associated with Harvard. But it took an 1880 poem by writer and Professor of Medicine Oliver Wendell Holmes to revive it for good. The poem urged Harvard to "let thine earliest symbol be thy last." If ubiquity is any measure, Holmes' poetic wish came true. Veritas was Harvard's oldest idea for a motto and, after centuries of neglect, is here to stay.

Search for truth is a tall order. Indeed, Harvard's search for its core principle did not come easy. (In fact, it took over two hundred years!) *Ve Ri Tas* is a high bar.

It's not unlike the United States and Thomas Jefferson's opening statement in the Declaration of Independence: "We hold these truths to be self-evident, that all men are created equal." That is an extremely bold claim, especially when considered in the light of the morals, norms, and mores existing at the point in history when it was first expressed. In fact, as many historians have pointed out, it was such a high bar that even its writer, a slaveholder, failed to live up to it.

At the same time, Jefferson's setting of the bar at such a high level established a critical legacy that has been perhaps our most important touchstone during our journey as a people. (Somehow, it's hard to imagine that we would be in a better place today had he written, "We hold these truths to be self-evident, that all white male property holders are created equal." That just doesn't have the same ring to it.)

Then, 87 ("Four score and seven . . . ") years after Jefferson wrote those words, Abraham Lincoln stepped onto a Pennsylvania battlefield in the immediate aftermath of 165,000 Americans having spent three days fighting each other to the tune of 51,000 casualties and more than 7,000 deaths. In our nation's most famous speech—a mere 272 words—Lincoln proceeded to echo Jefferson's words, reminding the world that our nation had been "conceived in liberty and dedicated to the proposition that all men are created equal."

Then, a full century after Gettysburg, Reverend Martin Luther King, Jr. stood on the steps of Lincoln's very monument, echoing Jefferson's very words with particular emphasis on the word "all."

Returning to Professor Steven Rockefeller, author of *Spiritual Democracy and Our Schools*, he writes:

> *The story of the founding and the nation's history since then raises disturbing moral issues and that moral complexity is being examined and debated today by historians as never before. However, contemporary reconstructions of American history will not alter a basic, long-standing principle regarding what defines an American citizen as an American. It is not a matter of religion, race, or ethnic origin even though some have tried to make such claims. It is a shared faith in the ethical and political ideals proclaimed in the Declaration of Independence and the Constitution with its amendments that defines an American as an American and forms our national identity. These ideals and values are the heart of the beliefs and rituals that some social scientists and philosophers have labeled America's civil religion. One can deplore the history of racial injustice, the brutal oppression of Native Americans, the inequality of women, and other ways the reality of American society has contradicted the nation's ideals, and at the same time embrace the American democratic faiths and experiment in democracy.*

At risk of understatement, *Ve Ri Tas* and Jefferson's vision of universal equality qualify for what Jim Collins (see his 1994 book *Built to Last: Successful Habits of Visionary Companies*) terms BHAGs (Big Hairy Audacious Goals). Ironically, we have repeatedly observed that one sign of whether such goals are taken seriously can be found in the extent to which they inspire humor and even irreverence.[1]

As an example, I annually compete in a circuit of "geezer" lacrosse tournaments for the senior citizen set. (One of our core principles is "We may be old, but we're slow.") Among the many college alumni teams that compete in this circuit is a team consisting of mostly Harvard grads. Their uniform is shown in Fig. 2.2.

It is common for opposing players to do a double take when they realize that the bottom word is not "Tas" but "Old" (i.e., It reads "Very Old" as opposed to "Ve Ri Tas"). On the one hand, it is conceivable that some old-school diehard Harvard stalwarts might regard the uniform design as disrespectful. On the other, when your students start making jokes about your mission, you might do well to take it as a sign that it has indeed invaded their psyches and they are doing a fair amount of thinking about it. (In the end, isn't that what we really want?)

Ve Ri Tas still matters in the twenty-first century and the effort to honor it is ongoing. At convocation exercises opening the 2022 school year, Larry Bacow began his last year as Harvard's president with the following words:

Our motto at Harvard is Veritas. It is more than a motto. It is the reason we exist, to seek the truth. But truth needs to be tested and needs to be revealed and that can only happen on the anvil of competing ideas. If you really seek the truth, it's important to engage with people who think differently from you. Even more importantly, you need to be willing to change your mind in the face of a better argument or new information. Only when you have this experience will you be well equipped to make a difference in the world.[2]

Figure 2.2   Harvard "Ve Ri Old" Lacrosse Team Player
Malcolm Gauld

With an espoused theory like *Ve Ri Tas* or Jefferson/Lincoln/King's statement on equality, you may well miss the mark more than you hit it. But that's true of all high goals. Great schools never stop reaching. They strive to adjust their attitudes and behaviors to match their mission. They rarely adjust the mission to fit the attitudes and the behaviors.

Whether you lead a school, a company, or an organization, assume that awesome cultures demand very high goals and aspirations. In my hometown of Bath, Maine, the sign shown in Fig. 2.3 can be found just down the hill from my house.

Bath is rare among New England mill towns for the fact that after three centuries it is still making the very same thing it has always made: state-of-the-art ships. Those of us who live here can often be seen wearing sweatshirts proclaiming: "Bath Built Is Best Built." (There is also one that reads "Frigate is Not a Dirty Word in Bath, Maine.")

Neither I nor anyone in my family has ever worked at the Bath Iron Works, but we join our whole community in sharing immense pride over the respect it has earned. We value the fact that Bath is known throughout the world as "Ship City," and everyone in town roots for the local Morse High School Shipbuilders.

Another example of core principles setting a high bar can be found in Rotary's "Four-Way Test of the things we think, say, or do":

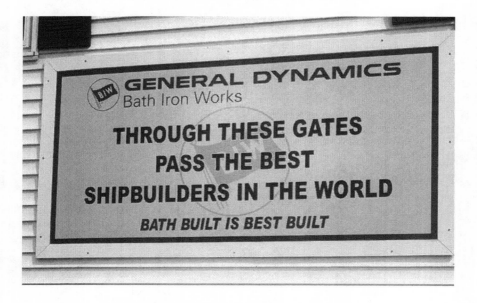

Figure 2.3   Sign at Entry Gate of Bath Iron Works (Bath, Maine)
Malcolm Gauld

1. First, is it the TRUTH?
2. Second, is it FAIR to all concerned?
3. Third, will it build GOODWILL and BETTER FRIENDSHIPS?
4. Fourth, will it be BENEFICIAL to all concerned?

Rotarians commonly express the sentiment of how much better the world would be if everyone lived in accordance with the Four-Way Test. It's not hard to see how it would inspire a sense of pride from any member. You might do well to keep that standard in mind as a litmus test for your own school's core principles.

Another example is the world-famous Maine outdoor outfitters store L.L.Bean. L.L.Bean's "Golden Rule," coined by Leon Leonwood Bean in 1912, certainly speaks to culture: "Sell good merchandise at a reasonable profit, treat your customers like human beings, and they'll always come back for more."

Of course, it's one thing to post some lofty words on a wall. It's entirely another to actually live them. As a graduate student, I was fortunate to take a course on interpersonal dynamics taught by nationally respected scholar and author Professor Lee Bolman. Bolman introduced the Argyris and Schon "Theory of Action." (See *Organizational Learning: A Theory of Action Perspective* by Chris Argyris and Donald Schon, published in 1978.) This construct holds that each of us balances an "espoused theory" (what we profess to believe) with a "theory in use" (what we actually do). Therefore, the goal of the moral, virtuous person *or* school *or* family *or* business *or* organization *or* community *or* country is to have the two dynamics coincide as closely as possible. When it comes to school culture, the leader has no job more important than guiding the school to a place where the actual culture (the theory in use) closely reflects the school's core belief (its espoused theory).

2. Common Language

Sometimes the core principle can be so "high falutin"—or, as is the case with Harvard, an ancient phrase in Latin—that some students, teachers, or parents will have trouble understanding it. That's where a carefully considered common language can be helpful.

There are countless factors worth considering in designing and establishing a common language. In our work, we have repeatedly observed a three-part commonality shared by schools with strong cultures. Specifically, they all seem to have found a sweet spot located somewhere between:

1. simplicity and complexity
2. consensus and reach

3. performance and moral character

An explanation of these three factors follows.

a. The Sweet Spot Between Simplicity and Complexity

When it comes to core principles or common language, a sweet spot exists somewhere between intellectual simplicity and rigor. Too simple is not inspiring. Too rigorous is frustratingly confusing. It is best to have a mix of both.

You also want to allow the students to come to their own understanding of the words in their own time. Avoid the temptation to restrict the students' understanding to a prescribed definition. Let them try the words on like a new coat and permit them to wear it around for a while. Let them make jokes about the mission or common language. Allow the concepts to infiltrate their consciousness without much regard for whether they even realize that infiltration is occurring.

The following story explains how one student negotiated the simplicity and complexity of our school's common language and found understanding during the journey.

James: A Common Language Story

In the early 2000s, a student came to our school from New York City who was a highly gifted basketball player. Not only had James (not his real name) experienced particularly difficult family circumstances—both of his parents had been incarcerated during his youth—he had grown up in a Spanish-speaking home and had little confidence in his use of English. Suffice it to say that his initial exposure to our core principle—"Every individual is gifted with a unique potential that defines a destiny" (as well as our Five Words: Courage, Integrity, Leadership, Curiosity, Concern; and our Five Principles: Destiny, Humility, Conscience, Truth, Each Other's Keeper)—was a lot to take in and internalize.

While James predictably distinguished himself on the basketball court in short order, he also worked very hard in the classroom and was an all-around positive role model for his peers by the time he graduated.

His success continued in college at the University of Maine, where he graduated as the only three-year captain in the school's history and was a statistical leader in multiple categories on the court as well as in the classroom, where he repeatedly earned America East Conference All-Academic distinction.

During the spring of his senior year in college, we invited James to return to our campus as the keynote speaker at our spring family weekend. During the Q&A session following his remarks, one of his responses to a simple, innocent question from a parent was particularly striking. The questioner asked, "James, remembering back to when you first started at Hyde, which of the school's words and principles had the most meaning to you?"

James smiled and then responded, "To tell you the truth, when I first got here I did not know what most of those words meant. I was seeing words in English but thinking about their meaning in Spanish. So, I spent a good part of that first year hoping that no one would realize that. I did understand Concern, Courage, and Curiosity, so I focused on those. Over time, the others started to make sense and I began to explore my life in accordance with them."

The faculty's first reaction to James' comment was that maybe we had erred in not taking greater care to ensure that he had understood the meaning of the words comprising our common language. The second reaction was: Maybe it—the simplicity and complexity—played out perfectly!

b. *Consensus versus Reach*

There is also a balance to be struck between consensus and reach. It can be an inspiring experience for a school to engage in a process where it determines or revises its core principles or common language. It can also put a school in an unintended straitjacket.

During a school leadership conference many years ago in Boston, Washington "Tony" Jarvis, then head of school at the Roxbury Latin School (Massachusetts), delivered a speech about character and schools. At one point, he said something to the effect of, "It is perhaps unfortunate that tolerance has evolved into the supreme virtue of our age." His remark captured everyone's attention to an extent that reminded me of those E. F. Hutton commercials of old where, upon hearing the words "E. F. Hutton," everyone in a large room of people stops whatever they're doing and begins listening intently for more information.

Tony let the message sink in for a bit before continuing (and I'm paraphrasing from a thirty-year-old memory): "Tolerance is essential. It is also the lowest common denominator of virtue. Being the one thing that everyone will agree upon, it can be a great starting point. However, as an ending point, it's inadequate."

His explanation had brought focus to thinking I had been doing at the time on *how to teach virtue*. At the time, I had been deeply influenced by the work of Kevin Ryan, founder and director emeritus of the Center for Character and Social Responsibility (formerly known as the Center for the Advancement of Ethics and Character) at Boston University. (Note: Ryan's one-sentence characterization of character education pretty much says it all for me: "Character education is not one more thing to add to your plate. It is the plate!")

In a 1999 *Education Week* article titled "Values, Views, or Virtues," he argued that many character education programs err by mistakenly regarding those three "V" words as synonymous. Arguing for a focus on virtue, Ryan writes, "Views, like values, can be good, bad, or morally indifferent." The problem with them being placed as the foundation of a character education program is that "character is somehow equated with being aligned with approved views, whether they are on race or the environment or how the genders ought to relate to each other."

Arguing for a "virtues first" approach, Ryan explains, "What distinguishes virtues from views and values, then, is that virtues are habits cultivated from within the individual and actually improve character and intelligence. . . . It is our virtues, not our views or our values, that enable us to become better students, better parents, better spouses, better teachers, better friends, better citizens."[3]

Returning to Tony Jarvis' observation, we tend to think of tolerance reflexively as critical in terms of accepting people with differences outside of their control: for example, nationality, race, gender, religion, or sexual orientation. That's a good thing. However, what about differences that are inside human control? How much tolerance should we extend to people who choose to cheat, steal, lie, scam others, or act as lazy slugs? How do we balance respect for tolerance when a peer or colleague chooses to blatantly disregard a school's commitment to personal excellence? (By the same token, how much tolerance ought we extend to someone with a deep commitment to personal excellence when it is paired with a complete lack of, well, tolerance?)

Whenever schools are considering words for inclusion in a core principle or a common language, "respect" and/or "tolerance" tend to surface in very short order. That's also not a bad thing. It may well be a good thing. However, it can become a bad thing if that's as far as the reaching goes. Any common language probably needs a lowest common denominator or two. Just make sure that it also includes a highest common denominator or two. The former without the latter will likely turn to uninspiring fluff. The latter without the former can feel unattainable. Try to strike a balance somewhere in the middle of the two.

As an example of the challenges that can arise regarding consensus versus reach, at our school, we have never heard anyone argue that "Concern" is a bad quality that does not belong in our common language. However, many students (and sometimes their parents) have voiced doubts about Truth ("Truth is my primary guide") and Each Other's Keeper ("We help each other achieve our best"). For example, they might say, "Truth matters but love is more important" or "I don't want to get up in other people's business."

Our job is not to defend our choice of words or justify their definitions so much as it is to facilitate an exploration of personal ethics, values, and principles within our students. One example of an organization reflecting this ethos is Outward Bound in its commitment to presenting its students with "values-forming challenges."

c. Performance and Moral Character

Before turning to some common language examples, the work of Thomas Lickona and Matt Davidson is pertinent to this discussion. Their 2005 book *Smart & Good High Schools* reports on the best practices in character education they observed during an extensive study of scores of schools. In their analysis, they delineate between what they call *performance character* and *moral character*.

Performance character might be understood as the excellence component. Davidson and Lickona write: "Performance character is a mastery orientation. It consists of those qualities—such as diligence, a strong work ethic, a positive attitude, perseverance, ingenuity, and self-discipline—needed to realize one's potential for excellence in school, the workplace, or any area of endeavor."

Moral character can be understood as the ethical component. They write: "Moral character is a relational orientation. It consists of those qualities—such as integrity, justice, caring, respect, responsibility, and cooperation—needed for successful interpersonal relationships and ethical behavior."[4]

As a 45-year traveler in the character ed lane, I see someone professing to be a proponent of character education strikes me as akin to a musician referring to themselves as a jazz musician. In response, I want to say, "That's cool. Are you into Bebop? Avant-garde? Dixieland? Orchestra jazz *á la* Count Basie or Duke Ellington? West Coast? Swing?" As a logical result of its very growth as a concept, character ed, like jazz, has come to mean many things.

In considering performance and moral character, it is important to keep in mind that they are, in the words of Davidson and Lickona, "interdependent." They write, "Performance character must always be regulated by moral character to ensure that we do not do bad things in the pursuit of our goals, and moral character always needs performance character to enable us to be effective in carrying out our good intentions."

In performance and moral character, Lickona and Davidson have formulated an important delineation. Schools intent on doing culture work will do well to ensure that their common language is informed by the moral and performance character constructs in addition to the simplicity/complexity and consensus/reach dynamics discussed in this chapter.

A Few Common Language Examples

While we are discussing the work of Davidson and Lickona, let's have a look at the "Eight Strengths of Character" outlined in their *Smart & Good High Schools* book:

1. Lifelong learner and critical thinker
2. Diligent and capable performer
3. Socially and emotionally skilled person
4. Ethical thinker
5. Respectful and responsible moral agent
6. Self-disciplined person who pursues a healthy lifestyle
7. Contributing community member and democratic citizen
8. Spiritual person engaged in crafting a life of noble purpose

It is easy to see that both performance character (e.g., numbers one and two) and moral character (e.g., numbers five and eight) are addressed in this construct of eight values.

Character Counts, a pioneer in the development of character education programming for schools, presents Six Pillars of Character. While this construct predates Davidson and Lickona's performance/moral dynamic, you can see that both elements are served by it.

1. Trustworthiness
2. Respect
3. Responsibility
4. Fairness
5. Caring
6. Citizenship[5]

Returning to the value of humor in disseminating a common language across a school culture, the same humor that those Harvard lacrosse alumni applied to *Ve Ri Tas* can apply to kids internalizing a school's common language. If you have seen the 1994 film *Dead Poets Society* starring Robin Williams, you may remember the scene where the students substitute the school's four words of *Tradition, Honor, Discipline, Excellence* with chants of *Travesty, Horror, Decadence, Excrement.*

Those students had to have given a fair amount of time and thought to the task of transcribing those words into such a similarly patterned sequence. Might their time have been better spent? Perhaps, but they will likely remember those words—both sets of them!—for the rest of their lives. And that's a productive outcome.

One School's Story

Hyde School, my own high school alma mater where I have worked for most of my professional life, provides an example of how a school's relationship with its common language can take the form of a long-running evolution.

Hyde was founded as a boy's boarding school in 1966 in Bath, Maine. It began with Five Words that remain as the core of the common language: Courage, Integrity, Leadership, Curiosity, Concern.

In the early years, these words were never formally defined, but alums from that early era recall the school's leadership and faculty talking about them endlessly. (Any school seeking to upgrade its culture would do well to keep that simple strategy in mind!)

Over the next couple of decades, efforts were made to offer some definitions, until a community-wide effort arrived at the presentation shown in Fig. 2.4.

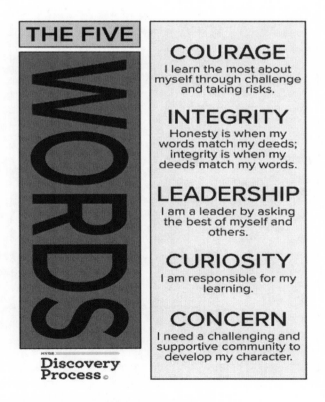

THE FIVE WORDS

Discovery Process©

COURAGE
I learn the most about myself through challenge and taking risks.

INTEGRITY
Honesty is when my words match my deeds; integrity is when my deeds match my words.

LEADERSHIP
I am a leader by asking the best of myself and others.

CURIOSITY
I am responsible for my learning.

CONCERN
I need a challenging and supportive community to develop my character.

Figure 2.4   Five Words of Hyde Discovery Process
Malcolm Gauld & Hyde Institute

Then, in the late 1980s, there was a feeling that something was missing. Alumni would speak very highly of how the Five Words had served as a formula for personal success. That was obviously a good thing, but there was a sense that insufficient attention had been paid to the notion of fulfillment and one's purpose in life. It was as though some were saying, *If the Five Words are my guide to success, how do I figure out what I want to do, who I want to be, or what my purpose is?*

This inquiry led to the formation of the Five Principles (Fig. 2.5).

While all of this work predated Davidson and Lickona's performance/moral character dynamic, that clarification is probably what the school was pursuing, perhaps unknowingly.

Returning to Hyde's core principle—"Every individual is gifted with a unique potential that defines a destiny"—some community members voiced the opinion that the Five Words spoke to the character side of the Hyde

Figure 2.5   Five Principles of Hyde Discovery Process
Malcolm Gauld & Hyde Institute

program while the Five Principles addressed the unique potential side of the equation. Then, one day during a community meeting, a young student raised his hand and observed, "You know, I kinda see it this way: The Five Words are what *I* need to do as an individual and the Five Principles are what *we* need to do as a community."

Out of the mouths of babes? Maybe, but that's what can happen when a student tries on the coat of common language and struts around in it for a while. In any case, we've incorporated that young man's synthesis ever since: "The Words are 'I' statements and the Principles are 'we' statements." Simple, but memorable. It also shows how good culture demands both individual and group effort.

Wording Matters

As an aside, and in keeping with the wisdom behind the aforementioned bus driver analogy, it may also be worth noting how the wording of our common language at Hyde has experienced some revision over the years. For example, when the Five Principles were first established in 1990, "Each Other's Keeper" was known as "Brother's Keeper." Not only did the story of Cain and Abel in the Bible provide an easily understood way to explain the moral behind the concept, but President Obama also gave the concept a boost during his presidency with his initiative of the same name.

However, over the years, questions were raised at Hyde about two factors:

Religion: *Is Hyde promoting some sort of Christianity agenda?* As we enrolled students from families who practiced a diversity of religions, we heard more of this. On the one hand, Hyde has always been non-sectarian and the story of Cain and Abel, regardless of where it comes from, explores the depths of the concept we were trying to teach as well as anything could. On the other, we worried that the choice of story might be a distraction detracting from the power of the message.

Gender: *Why isn't it "Sister's Keeper"?* (We did go through a phase where we used "Brother's" and/or "Sister's" interchangeably while keeping the word "Brother's" on the banners around school.) This sentiment may well have had some roots in the fact that Hyde began as an all-boys school and some felt that a decidedly masculine influence had remained in the culture.

While the religion and gender objections made sense, there was also some pushback we had not expected. Some students interpreted the term with a level of specificity that we never could have imagined. In other words, they maintained that the principle demanded that they be a keeper exclusively of their own familial brother (i.e., the one who lived in their home) but that they were not obligated to play that role for anyone else, especially when it came to people they either did not know or did not particularly like.

After much discussion, we decided to make the formal change to "Each Other's Keeper" in 2020. (It's not as easy as it sounds when one considers the full scope of necessary changes—to stationery, banners, publications, websites, swag in the school store, etc.—that must be made.) As the community settles into the change, many have taken to simply calling it "Other's Keeper." (As an aside, the folks who did not want any change at all seem to like the fact that the shortened form rhymes with "Brother's Keeper!")

Using that moment to consider other possible changes, we tweaked the definitions of one of the Five Words and one of the Five Principles as follows:

Integrity: The original wording was "I am gifted with a unique potential. Conscience is my guide to discovering it." Feeling for years that this wording was a bit vague and confusing due to the fact that it utilized one of the Five Principles to define one of the Five Words, we changed the wording to: "Honesty is when my words match my deeds; Integrity is when my deeds match my words." The students, in particular, like this explanation.

Conscience: The original wording was "We attain our best through character and conscience." This had long caused our English teachers to cringe at the prospect of using a word to define itself. (Some could be heard to say, "How can I penalize my students for doing it when the school does it on its own banner?") Thus, we deleted the word "conscience" in the definition and substituted "listening to our inner voice."

The point of this historical review is to emphasize that changes to common language require serious thought and deliberation. Do it at the first sign of disagreement and controversy and you run the risk of your school community never taking the common language seriously. On the other hand, resolute inflexibility can either fail to inspire positive engagement or can give rise to an underground common language as a counterproductive substitute. Again, somewhere in the middle of that fray, a sweet spot exists.

For our school, the experience of making these changes was a positive one for the school community. (Returning to the bus driver analogy, one could say that we tweaked the plan and vision without touching the mission.) It certainly served the purpose of supporting the aforementioned three objectives regarding the way our students ought to feel each and every day:

1. Known and needed
2. Safe and cared for
3. Role in shaping environment

Were there some diehards who disagreed? Yes, but very few. The other end that these changes served was the simple fact that it caused students and teachers to give deep thought to the common language. And that is exactly what you want to have happen in a school. The more attention paid and consideration given to the words in the common language, the more people try to utilize and live in accordance with them.

Impossible to Go Overboard

Once the words of the common language are established, it's almost impossible to go overboard in spreading them across your school community. Here are a few random examples of what Discovery Process schools have done:

- One year, the lacrosse coach had the Five Words emblazoned on the shafts of the team's lacrosse sticks.
- Discovery Process schools in Brooklyn and Orlando have the Five Words and Principles (and their definitions) presented throughout the hallways of the building.
- One faculty member has a collage of the Words and Principles on her office door.
- Another school has them covering the tabletops of the lunch tables in the cafeteria.

Use your imagination.

Beyond posting the common language in the physical sense, nothing is more powerful than recognizing, seizing, and capitalizing on teachable moments. Whenever a student, teacher, parent, or any community member acts in accordance with one of the words in your common language, stop the action and make a big deal about it. It might be a small act: a student holding a door open for a custodian dragging a mop and bucket down the hallway. It might be a bigger one: A student participating in a beach cleanup. It could even be a giant one: A student donating a year's worth of allowances to a local food bank. Whether big or small, celebrate it. After all, a common language cannot become real until someone acts out its words in real life.

At the end of each school year at baccalaureate exercises, some Discovery Process schools give Character Awards. Examples of actions and behaviors reflecting the Words and Principles are highlighted in front of the entire community. Is this largely subjective? Yes, but it shines a light on the common language in action and the whole community looks forward to this part of the ceremony. It is especially powerful when a student is recognized who is perceived as perhaps a wallflower but has actually been quietly and selflessly embodying the common language for the benefit of others. You can feel the community thinking, *Hmmm, maybe I could do something like that too.*

3. Practices and Traditions

Once the core principles and common language are established, they must be consciously operationalized in carefully planned practices, some of which will evolve into time-honored traditions. In writing this section of the book, I could not help but think back on some experiences from my own school days. Of course, at the time I was not thinking, *Boy, we've got some great culture stuff happening here!* However, the fact that I remember them over a half-century later would suggest that was indeed true. Here are five that quickly came to mind, in chronological order.

Table Monitors

In my K–8 elementary school, the eighth-grade students each monitored one of the lunch tables. It encouraged responsibility and leadership among the eighth graders and gave the younger students something to look forward to and prepare for. In fact, as a first grader, I remember both feeling that way and looking up to the monitors at my table with respect.

Periodic Breaks from Supervision

At the outset, I should probably disclose that as a lifelong athlete, coach, and fan, I harbor concerns about the current trend that I have come to refer to as the "AAU-ization of Youth Sports." (I should also probably post a "Warning: Digression Ahead" announcement!) On the one hand, I played Little League baseball, youth basketball, pee wee hockey, and competitive tennis before I even got to middle school.

The adult coaches I had for all of those activities were strong, and I benefited greatly from them. However, at the same time, the vast majority of the sports I played as a kid were unsupervised by adults and took the form of pick-up games during recess, after school, and on weekends. During recess periods, I distinctly remember the absence of adults. Maybe they were having a recess of their own. Maybe they were consciously leaving us to work on our interpersonal relationships.

In any case, we were left to ourselves to choose teams, keep score, call fouls, and settle disputes. In the fall, it was soccer and touch football. The winter found us indoors for basketball. Then it was baseball after the winter snow melted. Those were good times. They were also times of, well, social and emotional learning and development. So, this may be a long way of saying that sometimes the best teaching is no teaching.

Science Fairs

My elementary school years coincided with the post-Sputnik, pro-science enthusiasm of the mid-1960s. President Kennedy had announced that we would land on the moon before the end of the decade—and before the Russians!—and we all wanted to do our part. One of my sixth-grade class-mates was the son of a grocer. He hatched what seemed to me at the time to be a far-fetched plan where his father would refrigerate two eyeballs from a cow in his butcher department and give them to us so that we would conduct a dissection demonstration in front of the (undoubtedly horrified) parents attending the science fair. We actually followed through on this outlandish presentation, all the while believing that we were doing our part for the space race.

Chess Hour

In seventh and eighth grade, I attended a boy's middle school known for its academic rigor and strong athletic teams. Once or twice a month there was a school-wide chess hour. We were paired off by experience and ability, and the whole school played chess for an hour. It forced us to try something new and challenged us to develop our thinking and approach to the game. At the end of the year, there was a school-wide tournament that concluded with two students playing each other for ultimate "chess master" status with seemingly the entire school watching.

While schools might have big crowds at a basketball or football game, I submit that not many would get that kind of turnout for a chess match. The fact that everyone in school had played and had tried to improve their under-standing of chess skills and strategy presumably caused each student to have a deeper respect for what it takes to excel at chess. In any case, the respect in the room was palpable. (And returning to the "knowing what makes your school tick" point, this school was known to be especially athletic, even to the point of being referred to by some as an "incubator of athletes." Chess Hour changed the game a bit, perhaps allowing a different persona to take center stage in the school, always a boost to school culture.)

Door-to-Door Learning

Finally, I began high school in 1968, a year of blunt questioning concerning a wide range of social and political rights: Vietnam, civil rights, hair length, the environment, etc. Furthermore, as I began that year, not only were the brutal assassinations of Robert Kennedy and Martin Luther King heavy in everyone's hearts and minds, but people were trying to make sense of the wild protests that had occupied our television sets barely a week before the school year had started during that year's Democratic National Convention in Chicago.

At the time, the voting age in the United States was twenty-one. A teacher in my high school, new to the school that year, quickly became known to all of us for his anti-war stance. (We also thought he was cool for having been active in Students for a Democratic Society during his college years. Students for a Democratic Society was the best-known student radical organization of its day with a decidedly leftist stance.) He successfully planted in our heads the belief that regardless of our position on the Vietnam War, if the drafting age was eighteen, the voting age should also be eighteen. He organized a petition drive where we would join a state-wide campaign and canvas our town door-to-door asking for signatures to change the voting age to eighteen. Simply put, it was one of the most significant learning experiences of my high school years.

First, in the spirit of the time, we showed up wearing bell bottoms, tie-dyed shirts, and beads. He immediately sent us home to change into casual but clean and neat attire. That was probably the first time I ever heard the phrase "Take your job seriously, not yourself." (Note: The Humility module in the Discovery Process includes two lessons that speak to this saying.) He went on to remind us that our objective was to get signatures, stressing the critical importance of a positive first impression, especially when invading someone's space (i.e., their home) unexpectedly. Thus, in this case, our "job" demanded that we put our fashion preferences on hold.

Second, we met fascinating people, some on the other side of the fence of our beliefs. We even had some doors slammed in our faces. But we also got hundreds—maybe thousands?—of signatures. We felt exhilarated and celebratory at the end of the weekend.

Third, and best of all, we ultimately wound up enjoying the fruits of our efforts. Specifically, in the summer after my junior year (1971), the twenty-sixth amendment of the US Constitution was ratified, lowering the voting age from twenty-one to eighteen. Then, in the fall of my first year of college, I cast my vote in the 1972 presidential election. I was eighteen. Suffice it to say that rookie teacher did some great teaching as he acted upon his beliefs and took us along for the ride.

These memories got me wondering about the culture-inspiring experiences my colleagues might have had during their school days. Random conversations with them yielded many examples. Here are a few:

- A Maine high school conducts a daily twenty-minute reading period where everybody—both students and teachers—reads something of personal preference.

- A Connecticut school established "No Tech Tuesdays" where pen, pencil, and paper are the rule of the day for everyone.
- Another Maine school has every senior offer a casual talk during student assemblies throughout the school year.
- A Florida K–12 school organizes events and activities during the school year that match preschoolers with high school seniors.
- A Massachusetts school conducts a daily mindfulness meditation for its ninth graders.
- More than a few schools have school seals on the floor accompanied by traditions holding that students walk around the seal rather than step on it.
- Many schools divide students into one of two color groups where they engage in friendly competitions in a wide range of activities. For example, at my middle school, I was a Gray. Not only did we want to have more Grays than Reds on the honor roll during each marking period, but we also most definitely wanted to win the school-wide tug-of-war at the end of the year. (That was the thickest rope any of us had ever seen!)

I also reached out to friends and colleagues to learn of culture-inspiring practices and traditions at their respective schools. A few examples follow.

Annual School-Wide Hike

A Massachusetts secondary school begins each new school year with a community-wide hike up Mt. Monadnock in New Hampshire. The memories last a lifetime and alums of different eras have been known to compare notes upon learning that they attended the same school.

Honoring Local Citizens

Morse High School (Bath, Maine) annually gives The Mainsail Award (yet another example of the shipbuilding theme so prominent throughout the community) to a local citizen who has made outstanding contributions to youth in the local community. One meaningful aspect of this approach is that it challenges the students to transcend the idea that an award at school would necessarily be given to one of them. Instead, they need to think like the giver of the award, as opposed to the potential recipient, and give serious thought to those citizens in the community who have devoted their lives to their growth and development. It forces them to transcend the self-absorption that adolescents must ultimately rise above.

Hosting Special Olympics

A Discovery Process school in Pennsylvania has the entire middle school plan and implement a daylong Special Olympics event on their campus. The principal of the school described it as "maybe the most inspiring day I have spent as an educator."

A Look into a Ski Academy

During my career, I have been fortunate to chair several school accreditation committees on behalf of the New England Association of Schools and Colleges. (New England Association of Schools and Colleges schools are accredited every 10 years.) One of those schools was one of the pioneer ski-racing academies in the United States. A line from its mission statement speaks to its core principles: "We embrace an ethos in which hard work is held in the highest esteem and believe risking failure and learning from success is exceptional preparation for life." Upon arrival, a sign on the front of the main building supports this mission: "One School that Works." (Double-entendre intended!) These students and faculty work very hard. The fact that the school has produced (as of this writing) 118 US Ski Team members and 36 Olympians demonstrates that the program also indeed "works."

Lest anyone think that the results are due exclusively to careful recruitment and selection of talent, there is clearly a sense of "reach" demanded by some of the principles and traditions expressed in the school handbook. Here are a few examples:

- *There are no designated leaders—no class officers, no student council, no dorm proctors, no team captains, etc. Each person bears their own personal responsibility for finding a way to engage in and support the community.*
- *We do not believe in making "heroes" of our best athletes, best students, or best citizens, however these "bests" may be defined.*
- *Students and staff are responsible for the upkeep and cleanliness of the school.*
- *We especially value and respect work. We expect hard work in training, hard work in academics, and hard work in the community.*
- *Our community is committed to a philosophy of patience in helping young people grow. Human development (academic, athletic, personal) is a cyclical process. We respect that every individual matures physically and cognitively at a vastly different pace.*
- *Our school is not patient with laziness. Our staff and students have clear responsibilities. Hard work is expected in all areas of school life.*

- *We discourage the development of exclusive peer groups. For example, there are no senior privileges, junior proms, or different rules or standards for the best athletes. The school includes all age groups in all areas of school life.*
- *Our school does not give awards or prizes to selected students. No awards are given at graduation or other ceremonies for academic, athletic, or personal achievement, other than fun, intraschool prizes for periodic games and contests. We value equally the effort and growth of each student.*

One Size Does Not Fit All

Visit and explore the inner workings of enough schools and it soon becomes clear that activities, principles, common language, practices, and traditions that work effectively at one school might not have the same effect at another. For example, the "no awards or prizes" policy at the ski academy appears to contribute to a meaningful level playing field, especially relevant in a school full of students who share elite athleticism in common. However, at least two Discovery Process schools in Pennsylvania—both with inspiring student cultures—give awards for character and citizenship at graduation and find that the practice contributes to a positive atmosphere and strong sense of community. The differences in these two approaches to awards echo and demonstrate the importance of knowing your school inside and out and knowing the kinds of things that make it tick.

Hyde Practices and Traditions

When it comes to character education, Hyde School may be the only school in the country that is at least a half-century old that has never been about anything else. Character has always been our espoused purpose. Therefore, it stands to reason that our character education practices and traditions have been around for a very long time.

Here are five examples.

1. Introductions and Auditions

Each and every student and teacher sings a solo in front of the entire school community without benefit of instrumental accompaniment. New students get a taste of the auditions challenge—a warm-up, if you will—on the very first day of school with an exercise we call "Introductions." (See the Daily

Check-In module.) No one laughs at anyone else. (After all, you don't laugh at someone when you know your turn is coming up!)

After the audition, students invariably depart the stage knowing something about themselves—something good!—that they didn't know only a few moments before. Not only do performing arts build confidence, they reveal a sense that everyone is more talented than they think they are. But the greatest benefit is simply that students carry themselves better in their daily interactions with others. In fact, years after graduating, countless alums have verbalized a connection between a successful job interview as adults and the introductions and auditions they did at our school as teenagers.

2. Faculty Evaluations

Faculty evaluations are live. These are not the anonymous comment sheets filled out by students at many schools. Typically conducted once per year in the spring, they are direct verbal comments delivered to the faculty member who is sitting on stage—in a chair we call "The Hot Seat"—in front of the entire school community. (Some years we have divided the faculty and school into quartiles. While this approach can take away from the rich experience of having the whole school together all at once, the quartile approach allows for increased participation by students as well as more comments for each individual faculty member.) Once the faculty member takes the stage, three questions are asked of the student body:

1. What are the positive aspects of Mr./Mrs./Ms. _____'s teaching?
2. What does _____ need to work on?
3. Is there anything special you would like to say to _____?

History shows that there have been precious few occasions when students have deviated from the standard of constructive criticism without personal comments veering into personal attack. In general, the students are usually so "freaked out" over the very idea of adults with authority voluntarily placing themselves in such a position of public vulnerability that they are not quite sure how to respond.

The idea is to take what is already being said out in the hallways or outside of the building and bring it inside in the form of constructive criticism. It also shows the faculty modeling for students the critical idea that we are all works in progress. We know it has been a good session when, after the evaluations have concluded, we see multiple pairings of students and teachers engaged in further discussions. However, regardless of how well a given session goes, we invariably find a magnification of trust between students and teachers that, in turn, results in a stronger school climate and culture.

3. Senior Evaluations and Graduation Speeches for All

Given that Hyde is devoted to a philosophy and curriculum of character education, it requires evidence of character development as a prerequisite to a formal graduation degree. This standard of evidence is in addition to meeting the academic standard of passing the requisite number of Carnegie credits. "Senior Evals" is the key to assessing, respecting, and encouraging a student's character development over the course of their time spent at our school. At most schools, the month of May is a breeze for high school seniors, but "Senior Slump" really does not happen at Hyde. If anything, that is the time when students raise their game to its highest level.

If the Senior Evals process can be said to have a "gold standard," the Diploma is it. The Diploma signifies that "this individual is ready to conduct his or her life according to standards of personal excellence." During the evaluation process, the senior, peers, and faculty examine the extent to which the candidate has internalized the Five Words and Five Principles and attempted to apply them to their life. At the conclusion of the process, there are levels of graduation known only to the graduating class. The intrinsic value of the entire evaluation process rests on the assumption that honesty will be the guiding principle for self, peers, and faculty.

Then, during graduation, with their families standing in the audience, each senior presents a two-minute speech about what they have learned about their own character.

4. Even the Parents Graduate!

During Hyde's first decade of existence, 1966–1976, perhaps its biggest breakthrough in understanding character education could be captured in a slogan that has been said ever since: "Parents are the primary teachers and home is the primary classroom." Before long, another slogan came on the scene: "School is for kids; Hyde is for families."

In response to this breakthrough in understanding, the school set to the task of creating a program where parents would explore their own character development alongside their children in an honest and open exploration of three questions:

1. Who am I?
2. Where am I going with my life?
3. How do I get there?

On the morning of each graduation, a breakfast is held where the parents graduate. Each parent stands and hears a brief blurb, written by their own graduating senior, describing how the parent's participation has contributed to their child's education at the school. While the parent program has a number of objectives, an overriding goal is to help parents consider the idea that sometimes the best way for them to help their children is to become less involved in the trials and tribulations of their kids' lives and instead focus on improving their own lives.

5. *Everybody Does Everything*

In addition to holding down a full academic course load, any student who attends Hyde will also play interscholastic sports, perform in plays, do community service, engage in the student jobs program, and participate in the school's family education program. At many schools, the only students who play sports or perform in plays are those who are already good at those particular activities.

When everybody does everything, just about every student will have the chance to shine at something and every student will also have the experience of appearing unconfident or awkward at something.

The end result is a student culture where students feel encouraged to experiment with trying new things and there is less reason to feel the need to put on airs. It is also a student culture with fewer exclusionary social cliques. When the culture is working well, there is this powerful spirit that says, *We're all stumbling along together in search of our unique potential.*

ONE MORE: MAINE STATE LEADERSHIP DAY

In the spirit of Maine's state motto *Dirigo* ("I lead"), each fall Hyde teachers and students host a day celebrating the state's entrepreneurial spirit and what we proud citizens of The Pine Tree State refer to as "The Way Life Should Be." We have had as many as 1,700 students and teachers from schools across the state come to campus for a day of rotating workshops (each 25 minutes long) presented by doctors, farmers, fishermen, craftspeople, college athletic coaches, contractors, politicians, entrepreneurs, and on and on. Keynote speakers have included a governor, two US senators, a college president, and prominent business executives. Hyde students host all of the visiting students and cover most of the master of ceremony responsibilities. It's truly a high point of each year.

NOTES

1. Collins, Jim, *Built to Last: Successful Habits of Visionary Companies* (New York: Harper Collins, 1994).

2. Mineo, Liz, "Bacow Counsels First-Years to Be 'Slow to Judge, Quick to Understand,'" *Harvard Gazette*, 2022, https://news.harvard.edu/gazette/story/2022/08/bacow-counsels-first-years-to-be-slow-to-judge-quick-to-understand/.

3. Ryan, Kevin, "Values, Views, or Virtues?" 1999, https://www.edweek.org/leadership/opinion-values-views-or-virtues/1999/03.

4. Davidson, Matt, and Thomas Lickona, *Smart & Good High Schools: Integrating Excellence and Ethics for Success in School, Work and Beyond* (Cortland, NY: Center for the 4th and 5th Rs, SUNY Courtland, 2005).

5. Character Counts!, https://charactercounts.org/.

PART 2

Discovery

Chapter 3

The Discovery Process

WHAT IS IT?

Every School Has a Culture . . . Is Yours by Design or Default?

The Discovery Process is a school culture program designed for a target audience of middle and secondary schools. One might think of it as "Homeroom 2.0," a name initially considered as the actual name of the program. Students meet daily in mixed-age homerooms, share a common language, and participate as teams in various engagement activities (e.g., performing arts, intramural athletics, community service) throughout the school. Over time,

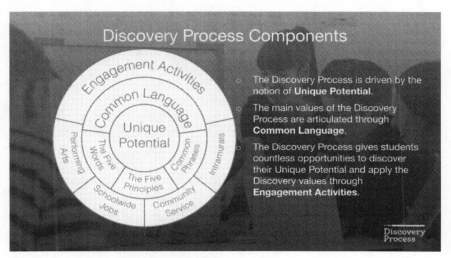

Figure 3.1 Hyde Discovery Process Logo
Malcolm Gauld & Hyde Institute

these engagement activities come to be perceived as co-curricular as opposed to extracurricular activities. (A popular Discovery Process mantra proclaims, "Everybody does everything.")

The training component includes more than 10 hours of online teacher-training—seven for teachers, three for school leaders—and is housed on a password-protected learning platform. It consists of 25 modules containing 134 social emotional learning (SEL) lessons and more than 50 instructional videos. Aligned with the Collaborative Alliance for Social Emotional Learning standards and Bloom's Taxonomy, the program reflects the character-based philosophy and program established at Hyde School fifty years ago and since adapted by a small cohort of public schools in the Harrisburg, Pennsylvania, region.

Our idea has its roots in a few deep beliefs:

- Every individual is gifted with a unique potential. Discovery Process schools are committed to helping children explore, discover, and develop that potential.
- Too many schools have devolved into a dispiriting mindset that says: *What you can do matters more than who you are.* We share the opposite view: *Who you are matters more than what you can do.*
- The Discovery Process prioritizes attitude over aptitude, effort over ability, and character over talent.
- It is built upon the belief that character is what matters most in both bad and good times. To repeat a phrase coined by Dr. Kevin Ryan: "Character education is not one more thing to add to your plate. It is the plate!"

In short, the Discovery Process concurs with the balanced form of education expressed by Martin Luther King: "Intelligence plus character—that is the goal of education." We also believe that for too long, our schools have been weighted toward the former at the expense of the latter and that the first step in reversing this is to put culture first.

The Discovery Process has proven to consistently deliver five benefits to fully participating schools:

1. Students feel safe and cared for with a sense of connection to school and one another.
2. They exhibit better coping skills in day-to-day interactions with both peers and adults.
3. A synergistic rapport develops between younger and older students.
4. There have been advancements in learning due to positive learning attitudes and sharper concentration.

5. Teachers have been enriched by the impact of the Hyde Discovery Process in their own lives.

The Product Suite

Each Discovery Process school receives the following materials and services.

Training Content: Individualized Training Program

Conducted by Hyde Institute staff, the training is designed according to the perceived needs of each school. We have come to campus and spent a full day with faculty. We have also conducted the entire program via Zoom. Sometimes we have trained the trainer who then trains the faculty. The online training program "lives" in a password-protected learning management system. It includes:

- One three-hour school leader training PowerPoint program.
- Two three-and-a-half-hour training PowerPoints for teachers, each containing more than 75 slides and more than 30 instructional videos.
- One Teacher Performance Workbook. The only hardcopy component of the training, the workbook is a note-taking tool that corresponds directly with the two training PowerPoints.
- One Online Teacher Handbook.
- One Online School Leader Handbook.
- One Online Facilitator Handbook.

Learning Content

This content consists of twenty-five modules containing 134 lesson plans. Chapter 5 ("The Twenty-Five Modules") presents a detailed explanation of each module and lists the titles of all 134 lessons.

Ongoing Training and Support

- **School culture assessment survey:** Distributed, tabulated, analyzed, and communicated by an independent third party.
- Monthly instructional **webinars** covering topics suggested by teachers and leaders at participating schools. (All are recorded and available at any time on the learning management system portal.)
- Access to Zoom training and support from the Hyde Institute.

How I Got into This

I began teaching at the secondary school level in 1976. Since then, I have been:

- a teacher in English, history, and music;
- an athletic coach—31 seasons of men's and women's high school sports including basketball, cross-country, football, lacrosse, skiing, and soccer; and
- an administrator, including thirty years as head of school and/or president.

During my time as an administrator, I was also involved with helping to found new schools across a spectrum of categories including private, public charter, and public magnet schools.

In 2018, as I neared the end of my thirty-year run as president of Hyde School and was pondering my next move, I visited a group of rural Pennsylvania public middle and high schools that had adapted aspects of the Hyde philosophy and program. (Specifically, the schools were in the towns of East Pennsboro, Halifax, and Upper Dauphin, just outside the capital city of Harrisburg.) In a word, I was wowed. (See the opening story in the preface.) The *esprit de corps* was obvious.

I came away from my visit with two questions: Could we develop and scale this thing? How can we not even try?

At the conclusion of this visit, Robert F. Kennedy's (by way of George Bernard Shaw) words were ringing in my head: "Some men see things as they are and say why. I dream of things that never were and say why not." These Pennsylvania schools had treated me to an inspiring view of things as they might be.

Things as They Might Be

Specifically, each stop at these Pennsylvania schools revealed an atmosphere of community where students:

- felt more included and had a sense of connection to their school and one another
- demonstrated confident coping skills in day-to-day interactions with peers and adults
- exhibited respectful rapport both with teachers and between younger and older students. (Specifically, I saw fifth and sixth graders looking up to seventh and eighth graders rather than fearing them, and I saw

seventh and eighth graders rising to expectations as positive role models and leaders.)

What's more, not only did teachers and administrators speak of advancements in learning that they attributed to fewer disciplinary distractions and sharper concentration during class time, they raved about the positive impact that the Discovery Process had inspired in their own personal lives.

I would also stress that I was given the run of these schools. In other words, while each school did set me up with a typical tour of the facilities complete with introductions to particular teachers and administrators, I was encouraged to go anywhere I wanted to go and talk with anyone I wanted to meet. All the stops on my visit showed schools where the "theory in use" was consistent with the "espoused theory."

Driving back to Maine, I crossed from New Hampshire over the state line at Kittery, where I was greeted by the familiar sign: "Welcome to Maine— The Way Life Should Be." I was feeling as though I had just received a view of how school should be.

How did these Pennsylvania educators get this thing going?

Origins: A Quarter-Century Ago in Rural Pennsylvania

It all started in 1993 on Bob Hassinger's first day on the job as principal of Halifax Middle School. By lunchtime, he found himself wincing upon observing some of his eighth graders cutting the line and cordoning off sections of the cafeteria where only they, the self-appointed "cool kids," could sit. Later that week, while accompanying his students to the evening high school football rally, he saw a number of behaviors that put a frown on his face. By the start of week two, he felt he had a culture problem on his hands that called for an out-of-the-box solution.

Around this time, a copy of Joe Gauld's 1993 book *Character First: The Hyde School Difference* found its way into Bob's hands. After discussions with Joe, Bob decided to create and implement a Hyde-based program. He began by transporting his entire faculty to Hyde's Bath, Maine, campus for a ten-day visit.

When they returned to Halifax, Bob and his team set to the task of reorganizing his school's homerooms from their traditional grade-specific formats to grade-diverse groupings called Discovery Groups. These groups did a fifteen-minute "daily check-in" (e.g., set goals, debrief the previous day, share supportive comments and constructive criticism) and engaged in a regular rotation of core activities such as intramurals, performing arts, campus cleanups, and community service.

The results of Bob's efforts were both immediate and dramatic. Within five years, Halifax Middle School earned Character.org's prestigious distinction as a "School of Character." When his students moved on to the high school, they successfully appealed to the principal there to replicate the program for their secondary school years. Furthermore, if imitation is the sincerest form of flattery, some neighboring communities (e.g., Upper Dauphin) chose to adopt the idea in their schools.

From the onset of establishing the program, Halifax and the neighboring participating schools set a pattern of tracking student behaviors and distributing evaluative surveys to a range of constituencies including students, teachers, and parents. The data they collected has uniformly spoken to the program's effectiveness:

- a 40 percent decline in disciplinary incidents over three years at one school
- an 85 percent parent satisfaction and 92 percent teacher approval at another
- zero playground fights during an entire school year at another
- budgetary cost savings due to fewer costly suspensions
- substantive improvement in reading and math test scores
- area substitute teachers who annually designated Halifax Middle School as their preferred assignment

As impressive as the results have been, visitors to Discovery Process schools are uniformly moved deeply by the *esprit de corps* within. After my initial visit, I wrote:

Although I feel I know great school culture when I see it, the uplifting atmosphere I witnessed on my first visit in 2018 would have been obvious to a rookie. One assistant principal described the Discovery Group as an effective arbiter between the student body and his office: "Every little thing used to come directly to me. Now the Discovery Group assists in steering kids the right way. This sends fewer kids to me, which, in turn, improves the quality and outcomes of the academic day."

Another sign of the effectiveness of the program can be found in the pride expressed by students and teachers. As one principal said, "We used to have a lot of fights here. Today, we don't even talk about bullying. It just doesn't happen here anymore."

In 2019, a summit of interested parties convened in Bath, Maine, for a Design Sprint, a formally structured five-day strategic planning process that one participant likened to "a strategic planning boot camp." We spent day one on a single question: *What is the problem?* By that day's end, we had our answer: *School leaders lack a tool kit to help them create and ensure a strong school culture.* We then made a commitment to build and distribute such a tool kit that could be accessed online by any teacher at the click of a button. We completed that tool kit in 2022.

How the Discovery Process Is Distinctive

While working on the final draft of this book, I had a conversation with Matt Davidson, founder and president of the Excellence with Integrity Institute, a friend and nationally respected character educator who is mentioned previously in this book. At one point, I asked him for his take on where the Discovery Process might fit in the character education/SEL universe.

Off the top of his head, Matt replied, "You guys remind me of a strength and conditioning coach for school cultures. And as is the case with any good strength and conditioning coach, if your clients aren't sometimes a bit uncomfortable, you're probably not doing your job. It's roots and fruits." Sensing my confusion, he explained, "You help educators get down to the roots of culture so they can do the work it takes to enjoy the fruits."

Today, there are many character education and SEL programs out in the educational marketplace. The Discovery Process is unique in at least five significant ways.

1. Culture by Design: In great schools, you can feel the creativity, effort, enthusiasm, inclusiveness, integrity, respect, and sense of responsibility. Such a culture only happens by design. It begins at "the top" and must be shepherded daily by committed teachers and staff. The Discovery Process provides a blueprint for doing that. That blueprint is available 100 percent online and is delivered in two parts: 1. training, and 2. learning content.
2. "It's not a program. It's a culture," said one participating school superintendent. OK, it is a program, but the spirit of the effort must guide the specifics of the details. How we do things matters more than what we do. When the program is fully operationalized, that "how" is in evidence both on and off school grounds. It can be seen at home in the family. It impacts friendships and activities within the larger community.
3. As impactful as the program's 134 lessons have proven to be for many students, they do not constitute the core of the program. The Discovery Group is the "engine room" of the Discovery Process. It includes mixed-aged composition, daily morning check-ins, regular

debriefing on activities, and an "Everybody does everything together" commitment.

4. "The How" matters more than "The What." At the core of the Discovery Process is a concept ("Every individual is gifted with a unique potential that defines a destiny") and three crucial practices: the Daily Check-In, the Debrief, and the Action-Reflection Cycle. While there are indeed specific modules devoted to each of those three, in order for them to be internalized by the collective student body, they must be woven into teachable moments at every opportunity.

5. 24/7 Support: In addition to monthly webinars on topics selected by participating schools, the Hyde Institute stands on call to help the program implement and troubleshoot.

Hidden Benefits of the Discovery Process

Earlier in this book, reference has been made to the goals placed at the top of my desk calendar each month describing the way our students must feel each and every day:

1. *Known and needed*
2. *Safe and cared for*
3. *Role in shaping environment*

And below those three objectives is a second of desktop calendar jottings:

Climate: Feelings
Culture: Collective habits

Every school wants these things. Fully engaged Discovery Process schools enjoy them because they understand, accept, and act upon the belief that Our Reach Must Exceed Our Grasp. This takes us back to the core principles mentioned earlier in this book. Great schools reach for more than what they want and this results in safety, respect, and responsibility.

They also tend to be the recipients of hidden or unexpected benefits. Here are five such benefits commonly experienced by committed Discovery Process schools.

1. **Immunity to Anxiety.** In her landmark 2021 book *The Awakened Brain*, Columbia University psychologist Dr. Lisa Miller refers to what she calls the "questing brain," a mindset that regards life as a journey of conscience and purpose. She postulates that the concept of immunity, one currently front and center due to the pandemic, is not limited to physical

illnesses. Her extensive research demonstrates that the questing brain can also assist immunity to anxiety and depression.

Dr. Miller argues that it is never too early for parents or teachers to help facilitate this journey for children. Whereas many SEL programs might claim to curb anxiety after it surfaces, an effective Discovery Process program can help counter it before it takes root. That is what can happen when a school perceives SEL as a preventative or enriching program as opposed to a curative response to problems.[1]

2. **Safety Is Necessary but Not Sufficient.** One of the first things we did when we began developing the Discovery Process was a competitive scan of SEL providers. This revealed a prevalent anti-bullying emphasis and a preoccupation with safety. To be sure, the Discovery Process believes that safety is crucial. However, schools shouldn't have to brag about it. Safety ought to be an assumed expectation. It's a means to an end and not an end in itself. Hence, by not having to worry about bullying or safety, you can move on to more inspirational things.

3. **Inspiration.** Even if an SEL program manages to make bullying absent, it does not necessarily follow that an inspiring *esprit de corps* will be present. Rather than start with what to do about bullying, the Discovery Process asks (and answers) a more holistic question: What to do about inspiration? Post-pandemic, a focus on anti-anxiety measures have come to accompany safety as a common emphasis of SEL programs. The best way to minimize anxiety is to meet it at its source with purpose and inspiration.

4. **Everybody Does Everything . . . and Learns More.** Angela Duckworth, chief executive officer of Character Lab, writes of the ever-present "trade-off that parents and educators negotiate between sampling and specialization, between exploring new stuff you know nothing about and getting really good at what is already familiar." Although specialization may currently be the order of the day in our classrooms and on our playing fields, we concur with Duckworth's assessment: "Early in life, when time is on your side but you know almost nothing, it's better to favor exploration."

Our national preoccupation with test scores—we call it "testmania"—in our opinion, has caused us to place sampling too far on the back burner of learning. The Discovery Process places it front and center.[2]

5. **The Best Possible You/Us.** Finally, whereas many contemporary SEL programs are focused on anti-bullying or Diversity, Equity, and Inclusion (DEI) curricula, the Discovery Process differentiates itself with its primary focus on each student's unique potential and helping kids become the best possible versions of themselves. While the Hyde Institute supports the efforts of any SEL program aiming to eliminate bullying and

integrate the important aims of DEI, we also proudly note that we began doing this decades before the terms SEL, anti-bullying, or DEI first appeared in the educational landscape.

A Few Words about Hyde

Priding itself as a private school with a public vision, Hyde School was founded in Bath, Maine, in 1966 by Joseph Gauld to test the premise that "every individual is gifted with a unique potential." An Advanced Placement calculus teacher and football/basketball coach in the 1950s and 1960s, he once found himself giving his highest grade to a lazy but very bright student with a poor learning attitude, and his lowest grade to a genuinely curious, classic "plugger" who exemplified all those personal qualities good schools espouse. Finding his beliefs in conflict with the status quo of academia, he founded Hyde School to test a new approach that would truly put character first.

Hyde began with Five Words—Courage, Integrity, Leadership, Curiosity, and Concern—and a cardinal principle: *Every individual has a unique potential that defines a destiny*. From the outset, the Five Words have served as the rudder of the program.

In 1988, Hyde added a compass with the adoption of Five Principles:

- Destiny—Each of us is gifted with a unique potential that defines a destiny.
- Humility—We believe in a power and a purpose beyond ourselves.
- Conscience—We achieve our best through character and conscience.
- Truth—Truth is our primary guide.
- Each Other's Keeper—We help others achieve their best.

These Words and Principles are operationalized by the Action/Reflection Cycle, a four-step process in which students:

1. engage in action: write a paper, speak in a group, run a mile, sing a song, etc. Then they . . .
2. reflect upon these actions both individually and in their Discovery Groups.
3. This reflection gives rise to a new view of self.
4. Students then begin to act in a manner consistent with this new view of self, continually strengthening it with further action and reflection.

The Action/Reflection Cycle can give birth to a dynamic school culture where all students study with enterprising curiosity, collaborate rather than compete, maintain the campus through a student jobs program, speak up in public, and test their personal leadership styles and capabilities. Furthermore, Hyde and the Discovery Process schools have uniformly found that when we put character first, strong academic learning follows.

As Hyde garnered significant national mass media attention in both print (*New York Times*, *Time Magazine*) and on television (*The Today Show*, *60 Minutes*, *20–20*), it began to seek ways to offer its concept and curriculum to public schools. These efforts included the establishment of public Hyde models in a number of cities in the United States. The Discovery Process is also a reflection of that commitment.

NOTES

1. Miller, Lisa, *The Awakened Brain: The New Science of Spirituality and Our Quest for an Inspired Life* (New York: Random House, 2021).

2. Duckworth, Angela, "Sample, Then Specialize," Character Lab, https://characterlab.org/tips-of-the-week/sample-then-specialize/.

Chapter 4

The Discovery Process *à la* the Bus Driver Analogy

The previous chapter discussed how the Discovery Process came about and the benefits it can inspire. Let us take a deeper dive into how it all works.

One way to explain the Discovery Process is to describe it in the context of the bus driver analogy mentioned earlier in this book. In other words:

- Mission = Core Principle
- Vision = Common Language
- Plan = Practices and Traditions

Beginning with mission, it's all about culture by design.

CULTURE BY DESIGN

If you are a school leader or teacher thinking about enhancing your school's culture, you might start with perhaps the most obvious observation of all:

Your. School. Has. A. Culture.

There's no way around it. You and your team may be ahead of the curve as you effectively guide your school's culture in accordance with an agreed upon mission and sense of purpose. That would be culture by design. Then again, maybe your school's culture is happening outside of your intended hopes and beliefs, thereby guiding you and your students in the direction "it" wants to go. That would be culture by default.

Figure 4.1 presents an example of the design/default dynamic. While it follows the dynamic encountered by Bob Hassinger on his first day as principal at Halifax Middle School in the mid-1990s, it is a dynamic that might present itself at any school in Any Town, USA.

Inspiring school culture often comes down to the interplay between the presence of particular elements and the absence of others. In great schools, positive attitudes concerning respect, creativity, effort, and inclusiveness are always present. Absent are bullying, prejudice, cheating, and indifference. However, schools need both sides of the equation—presence of good, absence of bad—in order to have a strong culture. In other words, just because the negative attitudes and behaviors are absent does not mean that the culture will thrive.

Many schools fall into a reactive trap where they might spring into action only when bullying and prejudice are on the scene. However, during times of "non-bad" culture, they may not put in the requisite time required for the more inspirational qualities that drive exemplary school cultures. It is important to remember that the students are always keeping their ears to the ground in order to figure out what we adults truly want, what matters most to us. If we end up reaching for a social and emotional learning or character education program only when we have a problem—and we never reach for one at any other time—that sends an unmistakable message to the student body: *Nothing says we have to be great. Just don't be bad.*

This dynamic is really no different from that which plays out in many families. Imagine the preteen who says, "Whenever mom or dad pulls all of us kids together in the living room, we know that one of us has done something very wrong." The same thing happens at schools. We reinforce whatever we

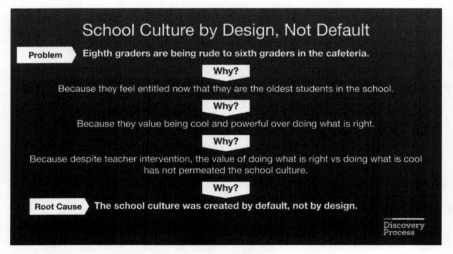

Figure 4.1   Hyde Discovery Process Training Slide
Malcolm Gauld & Hyde Institute

pay attention to. If kids always associate a new program at school with an adult desire to fix some kind of a problem, that sends a message. That message usually presents a barrier to strong school culture.

Again, inspiring school cultures are palpable to even the casual observer. Such a culture is no accident. It only happens with design. And the design begins at "the top" and is shepherded daily by committed teachers and staff.

Absent design, school cultures fall victim to default. There's still a culture there, but it's not an inspiring one.

The key, says Jared Shade, superintendent of schools at Upper Dauphin Schools (Pennsylvania), speaking about the Discovery Process, is that "It's not a program. It's a culture." And that level of culture is all about buy-in and commitment. It's about the school running the schedule as opposed to the schedule running the school.

School culture by design is easier to imagine than execute because school leaders lack the aforementioned "tool kit" they can access and utilize to help them ensure a strong culture for their students and teachers. The motivation to build and share the Discovery Process came from a desire to provide that tool kit along with a virtual track for schools to run on.

Right versus Cool

Thus far, we have discussed some of the barriers to maintaining strong school cultures. These barriers include:

- a now multi-generational emphasis that values what kids can do more than who they are
- a tendency for our schools to adopt agendas, curricular, and schedules in accordance with the expectations of college admissions offices, sometimes at the expense of the unique needs of middle or secondary level students
- "testmania" (my word)
- a tendency to regard culture reactively. In other words, when things are bad, reach for a program. When things are good or perhaps in the category of "not-bad," we might leave well enough alone.
- the COVID pandemic

However, there is another unique barrier, one that falls into the biological and developmental realm.

As they approach their teens, kids inevitably face a conflict between what is right and what is cool. Somewhere during those preteen and early teen years, the desire to please parents, teachers, and other adult authority figures begins to compete with the desire to impress peers.

Speaking personally, I can pinpoint a shift in fifth grade where getting laughs from classmates began to matter as much, if not more, to me than receiving praise from my parents, family members, and family friends. (Full disclosure: By middle school, my shift had accelerated to the point where I found myself in competition with my friends for bragging rights over who could amass the most after-school detentions!) In any case, the conflict between right and cool can lead to a range of school problems including disrespect, bullying, exploration of various substances, confusion over priorities, etc.

In recent years, bullying, in all its forms (physical, emotional, cyber) has been a major source of attention. Probably not coincidentally, many social and emotional learning programs have come on the scene amid the concern felt by parents, teachers, and school leaders. As has been stated multiple times throughout this book, that is not necessarily a bad thing. However, as one of my longtime colleagues has said, "Educational programs can sometimes help pull kids out of the gutter, but it's more exciting when they help them reach for the stars."

What he means is that there have been and will continue to be many programs that purport to help kids with academic or behavioral issues to improve and join (or rejoin) the mainstream. However, there don't seem to be as many that are designed to help kids—individually or collectively—go from good to great. It isn't easy for a school to make both the commitment and the changes necessary to create a culture where kids do not feel they have to choose between right and cool. However, those schools that have taken this step are invariably glad they did.

Core Principle: Unique Potential

Returning to the bus driver analogy, just as every school with a strong culture very likely has a strong commitment to a core principle or reason for existence, the same is true for the Discovery Process itself: "Every individual is gifted with a unique potential that defines a destiny."

Originally coined by Joseph Gauld in 1966 when Hyde School was founded, this statement reflects a belief in character development as the means to a fulfilling and inspiring personal destiny. We call that destiny "unique potential." As the quote expresses, every single one of us possesses that unique potential. It's not a competitive or comparative thing. It speaks to our purpose, who and what we are meant to be as people.

In his book *The Soul's Code* (1997), James Hillman presented an analogy of the acorn and the oak to represent human potential. Just as the tiny acorn holds the pattern for the huge oak tree, humans are endowed at birth with a potential for a future of unique possibilities and deeply personal callings. The

Discovery Process is offered in the spirit of that belief. After all, at best, there is only one thing that an acorn can become. Regardless of how we might choose to define unique potential, the development of our personal character offers the most promising path to a deeply fulfilling future.

Each of us also has character, and developing it holds the key to discovering our unique potential.

As Upper Dauphin teacher Adam Downing says,

Unique potential is this notion that every single student has something within them that will help them become the best possible version of themselves. They all have some sort of spark within, waiting to be ignited. I would be hard-pressed to find an educator who takes this on as a profession who does not believe that to be true in some way or another. I cannot imagine doing this job without holding that belief for every kid who walks in the door of our school.

Laura Gauld, president of Hyde (and my "better half"), puts it succinctly: "Unique potential is all about being our best, not *the* best." She continues: "We all have dignity and worth and we all have a unique contribution to make while we're on this earth. Therefore, we have a responsibility to try to develop our character so we can connect with what we were meant to do and the unique gifts we were meant to share."

Jason Stewart, a student of mine three decades ago, currently serves as president of the parent–teacher association at the New York City school attended by his two daughters. He offers a perspective on unique potential as a person who experienced the concept as a student and now lives it as an adult: "Hey, I didn't know when I was in high school that I would someday be the president of the PTA at my daughters' elementary school, but I am the president of that PTA now. My path led me here, and now I'm trying to do for others what was done for me."

It might be helpful to spend a moment on what unique potential is not. For one thing, unique potential departs from that well-worn phrase of encouragement that parents, grandparents, aunts, and uncles are fond of saying to young people: "If you work hard, you can be anything you want in life." We not only disagree with this statement, we believe it actually feeds some of our educational and societal problems.

Specifically, we have two disagreements with this statement. First, it isn't true. For example, I have both played with and coached scores of highly gifted and hard-working athletes who aspired to play in the professional ranks. While many of them live successful and fulfilled lives today, none of them has done so in professional sports. (And it's not for lack of trying!) Although parents have the best of intentions when they offer phrases like this, sometimes they are trying to reassure themselves as much as their children. More often than not, their children see through this. Sometimes they even think: *Mom and Dad like to say stuff like that so I won't dwell on my shortcomings.*

Second, were we really put on this earth simply to do whatever we want to do? I mean, to quote the great singer Peggy Lee: "Is that all there is?" Taken to an extreme, that mindset is both shallow and hedonistic. While I confess that I uttered more than my share of "If-you-work-hard-you-can-be-anything-you-wants" as a young teacher, I ultimately transitioned to something more along the lines of "If you work hard, you're going to end up with something (and maybe even someone!) you really like." I say it simply because I have seen it work out this way time and time again.

One of the lessons in the Destiny-Unique Potential module is called "Achievement Culture vs. Character Culture." The lesson is based on the premise that all of us (students, teachers, parents, kids, and adults) live in a world that challenges us to balance an achievement orientation with a character orientation. For students, the achievement side of the equation can come with indicators like test scores, GPA, or athletic statistics such as points per game or all-star selections. (For adults it can be salary, job title, zip code, make/model of car, or college alma mater.)

Indicators on the character side might include kindness, generosity, attitude, or community service. There are many pressures today that can find us preoccupied with achievement and success to such an extent that we give insufficient consideration to character and fulfillment. For example, ask yourself how many tasks or responsibilities you performed last week for the express purpose of helping yourself or someone else become a better person. Not only can a focus on unique potential help us sort out our priorities to balance out achievement and character in our lives, it can also lead us to understanding that the two objectives do not have to be mutually exclusive.

The Discovery Process assumes that a lifelong commitment to developing our character enhances our prospects for connecting with our unique potential. This commitment must remain steadfast in both good times and bad. Perhaps a poem by Charles Reade (1814–1884) best expresses the ultimate goals and purpose of the Discovery Process:

> Sow an Act and you reap a Habit;
> Sow a Habit and you Reap a Character;
> Sow a Character and you reap a Destiny.

Whether a participating Discovery Process school chooses to adopt this core principle or follow one of its own design, the Discovery Process seeks to help schools help students prepare to live lives of purpose.

Common Language

As discussed earlier, the common language of the Discovery Process is focused on Five Words and Five Principles. Figure 4.2 shows slide from the Discovery Process teacher-training program.

As previously discussed, it can be useful to understand these five words and principles as "I" and "We" priorities, respectively (see Table 4.1).

As figure 4.3 from the training program explains, the more the common language permeates the school culture, the more the words and principles guide the attitudes and behaviors of the students.

Integration is crucial. If students come to perceive the common language as a compartmentalized grouping of words that "we sit down and talk about every once in a while," there is little chance they will internalize it in their daily interactions with peers and teachers. (And there is pretty much zero chance they will take it home to their families and larger community.) If they hear reference to it and observe people actually living it multiple times during the course of the school day—in class, in the hallways, during athletic practices—prospects for internalization within individuals and the entire school community are greatly enhanced.

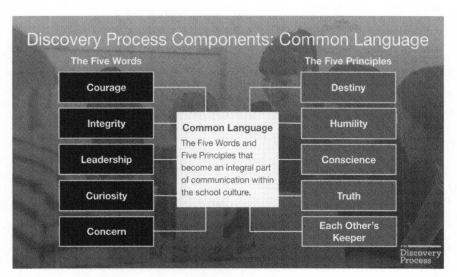

Figure 4.2   Hyde Discovery Process Training Slide
Malcolm Gauld & Hyde Institute

Table 4.1 Five Words and Principles as "I" and "We" Priorities

Five "I" Words (What I must do . . .)	Five "We" Principles (What we must do . . .)
Courage	Destiny
Integrity	Humility
Leadership	Conscience
Curiosity	Truth
Concern	Each Other's Keeper

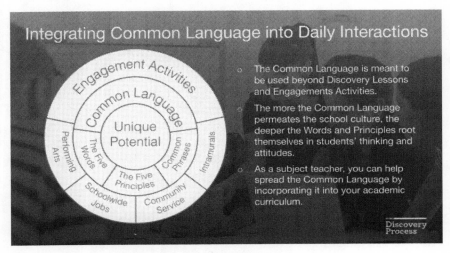

Figure 4.3 Hyde Discovery Process Training Slide
Malcolm Gauld & Hyde Institute

Common Language Turns to Shorthand

One sign that can suggest the common language is taking hold is the emergence of a colloquial shorthand in classrooms, in the hallways, and outside the building. Usually derived from daily life experiences shared by the student body, it typically takes the form of quick phrases. Here are some of the phrases that have taken hold at Discovery Process schools:

- *Is this your best?* (One school principal starts nearly every student discipline discussion or hearing with this simple question. Rather than explain what the student did wrong, he shifts the ownership of the discussion to the student.)
- *What is your conscience telling you?*
- *Leave it better than you found it.*
- *Character is what you say and do when no one else is looking.*

- *We cannot control how others react to us, but we can control how we react to them.*
- *Are you being a leader?*
- *This is who we are.*
- *Am I part of the solution or part of the problem?*
- *"Mandatory Fun"* (How the students poke fun at scheduled recreational activities. Some even use a word they invented: "Funishment!")
- *Our actions affect others!*
- *It's a right-versus-cool situation.*
- *It's constructive criticism with respect, not a put-down.*
- *What is discussed in Discovery Group stays in Discovery Group.*

While the shorthand may vary from school to school, its presence can usually be taken as a good sign that the common language is seeping into the school culture.

The Discovery Process devotes at least one module to each of the Five Words and Principles. However, these words and principles become part of school life only if students and teachers live them in their daily actions and interactions.

Practices and Traditions

Practices and traditions vary, sometimes reflecting a school's traditions common to their geography. As an example, some school districts in northern Maine have been known to begin school two weeks early in order to break in late September so students can help with the annual fall potato harvest. Schools in urban centers like Boston, New York, and San Francisco may be deeply engaged in causes supporting their respective communities. Schools in rural Pennsylvania might be aligned with the Future Farmers of America youth organization. As the figure 4.3 illustrates, four Engagement Activities are highlighted in the Discovery Process. These include:

- Performing Arts
- School-wide Jobs
- Community Service
- Intramurals

Some of these activities are common to any school. For example, all schools offer some form of gym or physical education, and usually some level of intramurals. The fact that students may play dodgeball, soccer, or volleyball is not unique. The unique feature of the Discovery Process involves the Debrief following the activity (see the Debrief module).

During a recent visit to Halifax Middle School in Pennsylvania (the school that launched the Discovery Process back in the 1990s), I observed the Debrief following a game of ultimate volleyball, a popular game that the school's physical education director invented for its intramural program. Sitting off to the side, I was extremely impressed by both the skilled facilitation modeled by the teacher and the level of attention and engagement on the part of the students. When I pointed this out to the principal, he replied, "Yeah, she [i.e., the teacher] is a product of the Discovery Process." Sensing my confusion over his comment, he continued, "She was a student in the early days of the program and now she has returned to pay it forward with her students."

This experience confirmed my belief that facilitation of the Discovery Process is a skill that can be developed. It's no different from what it takes to be a great teacher of mathematics or a coach of soccer: training, mentoring, practice, and evaluative feedback.

While **performing arts** is a fairly common activity at many schools, the Discovery Process adds a unique touch by encouraging everyone to give it a try. Some schools develop this aspect of the Engagement Activities to the point where students (and teachers!) perform auditions for acapella solos. Some schools even conduct them "live" in front of the whole school. Other schools plan for a spring talent show where students might sing, dance, or perform as individuals or in groups.

Also, five of the Discovery Process modules include lessons involving skits to be performed by the Discovery Groups. (See the modules entitled Attitude, Conscience, Courage, Know Yourself/Be Yourself, and What is Character?) We like to say that "every person possesses a ham factor." Performing arts can help propel that factor out of its common shell of apprehension. Beyond exposing students to one of the arts, performing arts activities have also proven to help students feel less inhibited in their interactions with others whether it be introducing themselves to others or public speaking in front of an audience of any size.

School-wide jobs provide an excellent way to foster school cleanliness and pride. To be frank, next to our recommendation for mixed-aged Discovery Groups, the concept of school-wide jobs probably receives the most "pushback" from prospective schools. The idea is simple enough: Set aside some time (such as two periods per month) when students and teachers will join together for a campus cleanup. Typical tasks include washing windows, litter patrol on the playground, sweeping floors, and cleaning up the auditorium following a presentation or the theater on the day after the school play.

Schools that commit to the school-wide jobs component of the Discovery Process invariably find that visitors will often comment, "This place looks great! There's no litter anywhere on school grounds!" Simply put, students who spend some time maintaining the cleanliness of their own learning space are far less likely to drop litter on the grounds or spray graffiti on the bathroom walls. Those of us who have created the Discovery Process program continue to scratch our heads, wondering how we ever got to a place as a country where the idea of spending a few moments to help maintain cleanliness would come to be perceived as a radical idea.

Community service is not a new idea. Some Discovery Process schools find ways to combine this aspect of the program with school-wide jobs. Some schools might even add a weekend activity for a cleanup of a local playground or city park. One rural school we worked with called off classes for a day to spend a day cleaning up the fairgrounds following a popular country fair. As mentioned elsewhere in this book, one Pennsylvania middle school organizes and hosts a Special Olympics track meet for area citizens. There are countless ways to serve.

Action-Reflection Cycle

A school's practices and traditions within the Discovery Process program are most effective when consciously conducted in observance of the Action-Reflection Cycle (discussed briefly in chapter 3). Figure 4.4 illustrates the progression of the cycle.

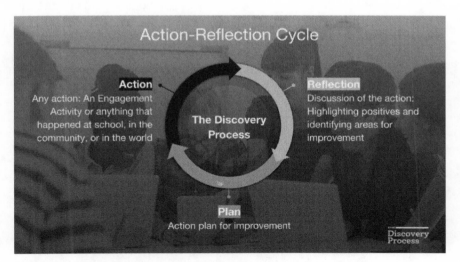

Figure 4.4   Hyde Discovery Process Training Slide
Malcolm Gauld & Hyde Institute

Once established, the Action-Reflection Cycle becomes a perpetual process of personal growth that can serve as a resource throughout our lives. (Note: There is a module in the Discovery Process called the Action-Reflection Cycle.)

THE BURDEN OF PROOF: ASSESSMENT OF SUCCESS AND SUSTAINABILITY

With a touch of irony, the Discovery Process might be perceived as an old-fashioned idea ahead of its time. In 2013, when Upper Dauphin, Pennsylvania, adopted the Discovery Process program, neither the students nor the teachers were clamoring for a new school culture program. A few years later, 77 percent of the students *Agreed or Strongly Agreed* that "the Discovery Program has made the school a better place," and 74 percent *Agreed* or *Strongly Agreed* that "my Discovery teacher and class genuinely care about my thoughts and needs."

In the beginning, it can be common for students and teachers to view the program unfavorably, only to become strong advocates once they experience its benefits. As an example, one can imagine that the notion of doing jobs or chores around campus would not be a popular idea. However, a year after adopting the program, 80 percent of the students at one Pennsylvania middle school agreed or strongly agreed that "school-wide jobs help us take responsibility for keeping our school clean and in good shape."

Similarly, at face value, the average person might not know whether Upper Dauphin Middle School's 367 incidents of truancy during a school year was good or bad. However, the reduction of this number to 258 in year three of the program suggests that something very good was happening. The same is true regarding student discipline incidents, which went from 509 to a low of 277 during the first three years of the program.

The most important part of a school culture is how kids and teachers feel about it and how hard they willingly work to uphold it. We aspire to a minimum standard of 80-percent approval (i.e.,that respondents reply) regarding how they feel about the following indicators at the conclusion of each school year:

- Physical and emotional safety
- Freedom of expression ("I feel encouraged by my peers to try new things")
- Friendliness
- Personal accomplishment
- My peers/teachers know me and help me do my best

Each Discovery Process school has the opportunity to participate in an annual school culture assessment survey that is created, distributed, collected, analyzed, and communicated by an independent third party. Students, teachers, and parents are invited and encouraged to participate. The survey results identify areas of strength balanced with areas that could benefit from improvement. It can then be utilized as a planning tool for the school years ahead.

Chapter 5

The Twenty-Five Modules

Discovery Process Modules

D 1 Daily Check-In	D 8 Truth Is My Primary Guide	D 15 Right vs Cool	22 Commitment
D 2 The Debrief	D 9 Destiny—Unique Potential	D 16 Embracing Difference	23 Profiles in Character
D 3 Five Words and Five Principles	D 10 Action-Reflection Cycle	17 The Best Possible Me/Us	24 Inner Leadership
4 Attitude	11 Know Yourself / Be Yourself	D 18 Rigor-Synergy-Conscience	25 The Biggest Job—Parents, Siblings, Family
5 Caring	D 12 Clear the Decks	D 19 Find Your Voice (Public Speaking)	
6 Courage	D 13 Concern & Each Other's Keeper	20 What Is Character?	
7 Curiosity	14 Humility	21 Conscience	Discovery Process

This chapter presents brief descriptions of each of the twenty-five modules constituting the first edition of the Discovery Process. These descriptions are followed by a listing of the lessons in each module. In some cases, extra comments have been added to highlight specific lessons that have come to be perceived by teachers and students as especially key "go-to" lessons in the Discovery Process.

Each module contains a six- to ten-minute introductory video and four to six lessons. In addition to being informed by the Five Words and Principles of the Discovery Process, each lesson has also been passed through a vetting process to align with both Bloom's Taxonomy and the five Collaborative Alliance for Social and Emotional Learning (CASEL) standards:

1. Self-Awareness: The ability to understand one's own emotions, thoughts, and values, and how they influence behavior across contexts.
2. Self-Management: The abilities to manage one's emotions, thoughts, and behaviors effectively in different situations and to achieve goals and aspirations.
3. Social Awareness: The abilities to understand the perspectives of and empathize with others, including those from diverse backgrounds, cultures, and contexts.
4. Relationship Skills: The abilities to establish and maintain healthy and supportive relationships and to effectively navigate settings with diverse individuals and groups.
5. Responsible Decision-Making: The ability to make caring and constructive choices about personal behavior and social interactions across diverse situations.

Each of the 134 lessons addresses at least one (and as many as three) of those CASEL standards. In each module, the lessons have been listed in order of difficulty and recommended order of delivery.

We are often asked, "Is there a sequence to the Discovery Process lessons?" The answer would be "No" and "Yes."

On the one hand, the program is offered in the spirit of maximal flexibility. Regardless of any sequence we might recommend, the cadence and issues concerning school life vary significantly from school to school. A school facing an outbreak of bullying will understandably be drawn to modules such as Caring and Concern & Each Other's Keeper. A school experiencing issues of racial conflict would do well to explore the Embracing Difference and Destiny—Unique Potential" modules.

At the same time, the Daily Check-In and the Debrief have intentionally been placed first and second for a reason. Representing the "how" of the program, they reflect crucial processes that effective Discovery Process schools utilize daily in conjunction with scores of activities: classes, athletic contests, play rehearsals, school assemblies, intramurals, post-vacation reviews, field trips, etc. To put it another way, any teacher who masters those two modules will likely adjust comfortably and effectively to the remaining twenty-three modules.

While those two modules might, at first glance, seem overwhelming or intimidating, both have simple questions at their roots. For example, the Daily Check-In is all about finding different ways to ask: "OK, Group. So, how are we doing?"

By the same token, the Debrief is all about finding different ways to ask, "How did we just do with what we just did?"

As the saying goes, the rest is just details!

THE MODULES

1. Daily Check-In

Perhaps the most crucial activity in the Discovery Process, the Daily Check-In provides the opportunity to take the collective temperature of the Discovery Group at the beginning of each school day. Its lessons are:

- Introductions
- Humility
- Flip a Coin
- Take Hold/Let Go
- Essay on Success and Failure
- Challenges for the Week

Regarding "Introductions," many Discovery Process schools begin the first day of the school year with a school-wide assembly where all of the students introduce themselves one at a time in front of all assembled. No judgments or shame. Applause is held until the last student speaks. It can be a deep bonding experience. Students who have difficulty with the challenge might simply be invited to try it again later in the year when they feel up to it.

2. The Debrief

Just as the Daily Check-in and Clear the Decks are designed to get a new day or activity off to a strong start, the Debrief is intended to add a finishing touch at the end of an activity, any activity, or at the close of a day. It boils down to someone asking, "OK, Group, how did we do?" Its lessons are:

- Attitude: 10 Percent versus 90 Percent
- Don't Take It Personally
- Character Timeline
- Group Mottos

3. Five Words and Five Principles

This module offers an introduction to the common language aspect of the Discovery Process. Rather than impose specific definitions on our students, it facilitates their efforts to "try them on and walk around in them a bit." Its lessons are:

- The Five Principles
- The Five Words

- Five-by-Five Mnemonics
- Five Words Inventory
- Truth over Harmony
- Aristotle's Golden Mean

Full Disclosure: "Aristotle's Golden Mean" may well be my favorite lesson in the whole Discovery Process program. It can be easily adjusted to use the words comprising the common language of any school and has proven to effectively challenge students to think deeply about their common language.

4. Attitude

Whenever we find ourselves facing difficult times, it is natural to wish for a different set of circumstances. This module helps students learn to face such times with a different set of attitudes. Its lessons are:

- Attitude, Attitude
- Identifying Attitudes
- Raise Yourself in Your Own Eyes
- Coincidence or Not?
- Skits on Attitude

Kids almost always get a kick out of "Coincidence or Not?" It also offers teachers the chance to slyly slip a bit of math into the mix of common language.

5. Caring

Members of a caring community both encourage and challenge each other. They do not use their time together to settle personal scores or reinforce cliques. This module teaches group members to show respect for each other and honor a commitment to the best in each other. Its lessons are:

- Leave It Better Than You Found It
- Emerson and Concern
- Not What, but How You Say It
- Find Someone Who Will Make You Do What You Can
- My Support Map
- Recognizing Our Strengths and Challenges

"Leave It Better Than You Found It" is a hallmark of the Discovery Process. "Not What, but How You Say It" can be a lot of fun and can bring out that aforementioned "ham factor" in your students. It can also serve as an awesome warm-up exercise for a drama class or for any cast at the start of a play rehearsal.

6. Courage

Courage is the first of the Five Words for a reason. Whatever our circumstances, our goals demand that we muster the courage to take that first step. This module helps students examine, assess, and begin to develop strategies for doing so. Its lessons are:

- That First Step
- Sharing Our Dreams
- On Courage
- Willow in the Wind
- Skits on Conscience and Courage

7. Curiosity

Most of us possess some level of curiosity about something. Most of us are also rather selective about applying that curiosity. This module helps students explore and develop the notion of enterprising curiosity as well as the habit of actively pursuing the answers. Its lessons are:

- Owning My Learning
- Curiosity Quotes
- The Lighthouse Story
- If You Can't Get Out of It, Get into It
- Know Yourself, Be Yourself: Moral Dilemmas

"The Lighthouse Story," borrowed from Stephen Covey's book *The 7 Habits of Highly Effective People* (1989), has closed out many a parents' weekend at Hyde School. We've been utilizing it for more than three decades, and it never fails to evoke thoughtful reactions. "If You Can't Get Out of It, Get into It" is a timeless Discovery Process mantra.

8. Truth Is My Primary Guide

Truth alone will not produce genuine character development. (It would also make for a brutal school climate.) However, it may be the most crucial element in individual or group character growth. This module can help keep truth at the forefront of the Discovery Process. Its lessons are:

- Life Is Hard
- Don't Lie; Don't Quit
- Who Am I?
- The 7–11 Dilemma—What Would You Do?
- The Truth Grid
- Skits on Conscience

"Don't Lie; Don't Quit" has been a Discovery Process mantra since the program's inception. I came up with "The 7–11 Dilemma" on the spot during a school assembly in the mid-1980s. I have since shared it with thousands of teenagers across the United States. The premise is simple enough: *What do you do when the cash register clerk at the store gives you back too much change?* The responses never fail to trigger a fully charged discussion.

9. Destiny–Unique Potential

At the core of the Discovery Process is the belief that "every individual is gifted with a unique potential that defines a destiny." Furthermore, our personal character is the key to that potential. This module introduces this idea. Its lessons are:

- Who Will I Be This Year?
- Achievement Culture versus Character Culture
- Character Aspects of Defining Moments
- Guess the Hero Game
- Share a Hero

As the introduction of this book indicates, those of us who have devoted our energies to developing the Discovery Process believe that our schools and the motivations for improving them are currently being driven by an "Achievement Culture" (grades, money, status, etc.) while a "Character Culture" (kindness, honesty, purpose, etc.) makes suggestions from the back seat. It's time to switch drivers. This module helps students explore that dynamic.

10. Action-Reflection Cycle

This module introduces a four-stage process of personal growth where students act, reflect (on their action), visualize a new view of self, and act in accordance with this new view, thereby establishing a chain reaction of ongoing action-reflection. Its lessons are:

- Attitude/My Attitudes
- Act Your Way into Feeling
- The Chair Exercise
- Thank-You Letter
- Charlie Everybody
- Learning from Lobsters

If the teacher can muster their own ham factor, "The Chair Exercise" can be a big hit with students. Perhaps it makes sense that a program that traces its earliest roots back to Maine might have a lesson called "Learning from Lobsters." Not only does Eda LeShan's (1922–2002) "Lobster Story" never fail to make a deep impression on kids, it often leaves a bigger one with adults.

11. Know Yourself, Be Yourself

This module helps students understand more about their own strengths and challenges while finding the courage to be themselves. It is guided by three tenets: 1. We are all unique and aspire to be somebody of dignity and worth. 2. It takes courage to be ourselves. 3. We need to be supported and challenged by others. Its lessons are:

- Sow a Habit, Reap a Character
- The Sign Exercise
- Labels We Wear
- What Is Unique Potential
- Discussion Exercise followed by Skits

"Sow a Habit, Reap a Character" borrows from the famous poem on character by novelist Charles Reade (1814–1884).

12. Clear the Decks

In any grouping of humans, it is not uncommon for the simplest of personal issues to fester into uncomfortable and unproductive resentments. A little bit of "Clear the Decks" on the front end can prevent the harsh unleashing of resentments (and hurtful gossip) on the back end while contributing to a closer group throughout. Its lessons are:

- Know Thy Kryptonite
- Public Self, Private Self
- Stop-Start-Continue

- I Know Our Group Is Working When . . .
- Character Reflexes

Although I originally coined "Know Thy Kryptonite" as a piece of advice for college-bound high school seniors in my first *College Success Guaranteed* book, this has been revised to also apply to younger audiences. Both "Stop-Start-Continue" and "I Know Our Group Is Working When . . . " can be utilized repeatedly during any school year. (They can also serve to liven up a boring faculty meeting!)

13. Concern and Each Other's Keeper

Discovery Process students look out for each other. The Each Other's Keeper principle states: "We help others achieve their best." Each Other's Keeper has been explained as the proper balance "between a bear hug and a kick in the pants." This module can help students differentiate the fine line dividing genuine caring and "getting up in each other's business." Its lessons are:

- Intentional Kindness
- Each Other's Keeper: What Would You Do?
- Anonymous Challenges
- Quotes on Each Other's Keeper
- We Support the Best in Each Other

Many students find Each Other's Keeper to be the hardest of all the Discovery Process concepts to understand and/or accept. Many alumni of the program consider it the glue that holds the culture together. It demands patience from the teacher as it seeps into the culture over time.

14. Humility

Rugged individualism is such a prevalent theme in films (and in portrayals of the heroes of our pop culture) that humility is sometimes perceived as a sign of weakness. We are not islands. On the road to success, nobody gets to the destination alone, no matter what might happen in the movies. This module encourages students to value humility in their lives. Its lessons are:

- Don't Take Yourself Too Seriously
- Got Humility?
- Take Your Job Seriously, Not Yourself
- If You Stand for Nothing, You'll Fall for Anything
- Our Greatest Fear

Humility is another tough one for both the teacher and the student. One of my go-to lines is "Humility does not mean thinking less of yourself. It means thinking of yourself less."

15. Right versus Cool

It is common for adolescents to feel conflicted between what is right and what is cool. This module presents lessons designed to help them with that balancing act. Its lessons are:

- A Higher Vision
- Sentence Completion
- Seek to Understand
- Zig or Zag?
- Iceberg Exercise
- Henry Ford's Best Friend

"Right versus Cool" is a term first coined by Bob Hassinger, founder of the first Discovery Process program at Halifax Middle School in Pennsylvania. History has shown that "Zig or Zag?" and the "Iceberg Exercise" tend to be well received by students.

16. Embracing Difference

More than two hundred years ago, the US Congress affixed the motto *E pluribus unum* ("Out of many, one") to the Great Seal of the United States. It has proven a difficult concept for people to comprehend and act upon during the last two-plus centuries. This module presents lessons designed to help students and teachers internalize the critical connection between their own unique potential (the "one") and that of their Discovery Group members, their schoolmates, and members of their larger community (the "many.") Its lessons are:

- "I Have a Dream . . . "
- MLK Day
- Inclusion and Exclusion
- P.A.C.E. (People Are Created Equal) Journaling
- Look Beyond the Surface
- What Would You Do?

This module has been especially effective for teachers seeking to incorporate journaling into their social and emotional learning work.

17. The Best Possible Me/Us

Discovery Process schools believe it is essential for students to have an understanding of their own personal best, irrespective of anyone else's. This module helps students and their teachers explore this idea, which can be unfamiliar territory for students who have been immersed in a traditional, GPA-conscious environment. Its lessons are:

- Give'em Seven
- Of Eagles and Turkeys
- Create Effort Savings Bank
- Excellence, Efforts, Motions, Off-Track
- Play the Hand You're Dealt
- Fleming's Law

"Create Effort Savings Bank" might be best suited to older high school students, but many Discovery Process alums have been known to refer to it long after their school days are over.

18. Rigor-Synergy-Conscience

Rigor-Synergy-Conscience is a three-stage construct reflecting the evolution of personal growth and development in all people. Rigor reflects our initiative and striving to do our best. Synergy encompasses our capacity to ally and work with others. (A popular Discovery Process formula for defining synergy is "1 + 1 = 3.") Conscience reflects our inner moral guidance system. This module makes reference to all three stages of the construct. Its lessons are:

- The Butterfly Story
- Luck and Hard Work
- Building Blocks
- Intellectual, Physical, Social, Emotional, Spiritual (IPSES) Challenge
- Big Picture/Little Picture

"The Butterfly Story" may have a bigger impact on parents than on students. "Luck and Hard Work" addresses the notion of performance character discussed earlier in this book.

19. Find Your Voice (Public Speaking)

Watch any group of children engaged in nearly any activity on a school playground and you will see the key ingredient for effective public speaking. We call it the "playground voice." This module introduces students and teachers to the basic elements—skills, techniques, attitudes—composing the playground voice. Its lessons are:

- Breathe . . . Then Speak
- My Body Language
- My Speaking Control
- Your Playground Voice
- Putting It All Together

Some Discovery Process schools—Hyde, especially—offer full programs devoted to public speaking. This module is a basic introduction.

20. What Is Character?

This question may be the cousin of the question, What Is Life? No one knows for sure. There is an endless reservoir of quotes on the subject, many of them anonymous. This module is designed to help you begin to develop a definition that works for you. Its lessons are:

- What Is Character?
- What Word Do You Need to Focus On?
- Something for Nothing
- Moral Compass
- Skits on Words and Principles

"Moral Compass" can be a powerful exercise for students of any age. Even if a younger student can't quite "get it," do not underestimate the power of simply planting an idea in a young person's head, where it can develop over time.

21. Conscience

Emerging teenagers stand at a unique crossroads where they strive to balance the urge to pursue primitive wants with a newer, perhaps unfamiliar voice counseling truth and a higher purpose. This module introduces students to the idea that active conscience not only empowers all of us to hear our deepest inner voice, but it inspires us to follow its lead. Its lessons are:

- My Conscience Is My Guide
- Quotes on Conscience
- What Does Conscience Mean to Me?

- Unique Potential Visual Exercise
- Executive Function

Regarding the "Executive Function" lesson, during my days as a teacher of history and government, in casual interactions with my students I would sometimes ask, "So, how are you coming along with your executive function?" I would then use their puzzled expressions as an opportunity to teach a little government. I came up with this lesson in hopes of personalizing the teaching of the three branches of the US federal government: 1. Executive, 2. Legislative, and 3. Judicial. (Once we cover the executive function, the legislative focus speaks to one's ability to forge effective and mutually beneficial alliances while the judicial emphasis can help students explore their understandings and tendencies concerning justice toward others.)

22. Commitment

A popular anonymous quote sums up the focus of this module: "Commitment means staying loyal to what you said you were going to do long after the mood you said it in has left you." Commitments are easy to make and hard to keep. It can be extremely difficult to maintain our commitments when we are going through periods of limited or no discernible progress or when no one else encourages, let alone notices, our efforts. Commitment is what pulls us through. It is the only thing that has the power to make the seemingly impossible possible. This module, like much of the Discovery Process, seeks to nurture a respect for commitment as a powerful life force. Its lessons are:

- Press On
- The One Thing
- Flash and Slow Power
- "Until One Is Committed . . . "
- Success/Failure Collages

"Flash and Slow Power" explores my personal story as a young and aspiring athlete. "The One Thing" is a time-honored Discovery Process concept that can be useful to anyone of any age.

23. Profiles in Character

This module borrows from the title and theme of President John F. Kennedy's acclaimed book *Profiles in Courage* (1956) and tells the true stories of people who are now adults—real people, changed names—who once attended Discovery Process schools. The goal of each is to have the students "walk in the shoes" of these individuals, and ponder how they might react in circumstances similar to the ones they faced. Its lessons are:

- Courage to Try
- Knowing When to Change Course and Let Go
- Basketball Dreams
- Hide of an Elephant, Heart of a Butterfly
- Unsung Heroes

"Unsung Heroes" can be utilized several times during a school year. Not only is it a great way to recognize those kids who often fall through the cracks of school life, it can highlight the efforts of those who step outside of their comfort zones. Examples include the athlete who tries out for the school play, the artist who joins the soccer team, and the quiet student who picks up litter on school grounds.

24. Inner Leadership

As Pearl Kane, who founded and directed The Klingenstein Program at Teachers College, Columbia University, was fond of saying, "Leadership is a behavior, not a position." This module is a condensed version of the full curriculum of a Hyde School character education course of the same name. It offers an introduction to the notion of developing one's sense of "leadership from the inside out." Central to the Discovery Process is the tenet that we all possess a potential Inner Leader across five domains: Self-Awareness, Public-Speaking Confidence, Tackling Challenges outside of Our Comfort Zone, Meaningful Relationships, and Family Context. Its lessons are:

- Tackling Challenges outside Our Comfort Zone
- Public-Speaking Confidence
- Journaling Questions on Inner Leadership
- Self-Awareness
- Meaningful Relationships
- Family Context

Hyde School has developed this focused curriculum as a way to address a perceived need for what might be considered an "Advanced Character Education" option.

25. The Biggest Job: Parents, Siblings, Family

The Biggest Job is shorthand for *The Biggest Job We'll Ever Have* (2001), a book on character-based parenting written by myself and Laura Gauld. The book and its Ten Priorities present the belief that "The parent is the primary teacher and home is the primary classroom." True character development efforts at school require a bridge between home and school. Hence, the Biggest Job module provides an opening for the family to enter the mix and participate in the Discovery Process. Its lessons are:

- Home Self versus School Self
- Roles in the Family
- The Family Shield
- The Wizard of Oz
- Each Other's Keeper and Family Scenarios
- Inspiration: Job 1

The Biggest Job module brings the student's family into the mix. The Hyde Institute has developed a full program for parents.

THREE SAMPLE LESSONS

Each lesson follows the following sequential format:

- **Title**
- **Overview**: A few sentences of explanation
- **Social Emotional Learning Connection**: Each lesson has been aligned with at least one (but not more than three) of the five CASEL standards.
- **Learning Objectives**: Each lesson has been aligned with the structure of Bloom's Taxonomy.
- **Materials Needed**
- **Activity**: For the benefit of the teacher, a detailed description/explanation of the activity is given.
- **Reflection/Closing**: A few closing questions are given to the students to consider.
- **Readings**: Some lessons include brief readings to share with the students.

Sample Lesson 1: Stop-Start-Continue
Module: Clear the Decks

One of five lessons in the Clear the Decks module, "Stop-Start-Continue" is the "go-to" lesson for many teachers, coaches, and administrators in the Discovery Process. It can be utilized in countless circumstances repeatedly during the course of a school year. It is also a great stand-alone debriefing technique.

Sample Lesson 2: The 7–11 Dilemma—What Would You Do?

Module: Truth Is My Primary Guide

This previously referenced moral dilemma lesson has been shared with thousands of teenagers over the past three decades. Unlike "Stop-Start-Continue," it probably works best as a once-a-year exercise, but students have been known to give different answers over time as they mature.

Sample Lesson 3: Aristotle's Golden Mean Module: Five Words and Five Principles

Simply put, I have never found anything better when it comes to challenging students on their understanding of character-based words that they may well have heard throughout their lives but taken for granted.

I was introduced to the idea at the annual Character.org conference in Washington by Marvin Berkowitz, the inaugural Sanford N. McDonnell Endowed Professor of Character Education at the University of Missouri–St. Louis. I had always wanted to hear Marvin speak and was particularly interested when I heard his presentation on the idea of applying Aristotle's Golden Mean to character education.

Aristotle's construct defines moral behavior as the mean between two extremes—deficiency at one end, excess at the other. For example, courage, one of the words in the Discovery Process common language, might be represented as cowardice in the deficient extreme and foolhardiness or recklessness in the excess extreme.

When I returned to our school, I decided to "feed" the Five Words and Principles through Aristotle's filter. After a session with our seniors and another with a group of our faculty, here is where we landed:

Vice of **Deficiency**	Golden Mean	Vice of **Extreme**
Cowardice	COURAGE	Reckless
Dishonest	INTEGRITY	Self-righteous
Meek and invisible	LEADERSHIP	Domineering
Disinterested	CURIOSITY	Dilettante
Cruelty	CONCERN	Enabling
Hedonist	DESTINY	Narcissist
Superiority complex	HUMILITY	Inferiority complex
Evil	CONSCIENCE	Psychotic
Liar	TRUTH	Self-righteous
Uncaring	EACH OTHER'S KEEPER	Co-dependent

Perhaps the greatest value derived from this lesson is the extent to which students stretch their minds in thinking about the deeper meaning of each of these ten concepts. It also compels them to channel their inner thesaurus, which English teachers tend to like!

WHAT THE LESSONS ARE AND . . . ARE NOT

Over a two-year period, colleagues at the Hyde Institute spent countless hours of time and energy assembling and presenting the 134 lessons comprising the first edition of the Discovery Process. We scoured through decades of materials we had seen teachers effectively utilize in the past, selecting the best and discarding the rest. We gave serious consideration to determining the extent to which the effectiveness we might have observed in the past had been due to the construct of the lesson versus how much it might have been due to the simple fact that it was being delivered by an exceptional teacher, one who could conceivably hold students in rapt attention while teaching the phone book (Remember phone books?). We wanted to end up with a set of lessons that would prove useful to teachers of any experience and ability level.

We also reached out to other educators we respected for reinforcement, especially when we neared the end of our work and realized that certain modules were light on lessons. Then we revised and edited the materials, constantly critiquing each other's work. Finally, we checked that the lessons reflected Bloom's Taxonomy and the CASEL standards.

Although we care about depth more than breadth, we believe that the lessons add up to a solid balanced model for a strong character ed/SEL program.

But the lessons by themselves are not the Discovery Process.

The heart of the program lies in the Discovery Group. It's in the daily check-Ins, the debriefs, the sharing of hopes and challenges. For sure, a commitment to the Discovery Group model will make for a better school year and a stronger culture. But the potential of the Discovery Group far exceeds those rather modest objectives.

Earlier, I told the story of watching an excellent post-intramurals debrief only to learn that the facilitating teacher turned out to be an alumnus of that school who had been one of the early Discovery Process school graduates. In a similar vein, Bob Hassinger, the former superintendent of the Halifax, Pennsylvania, schools who established the first Discovery Process program at Halifax Middle School, tells this story:

> *One high school senior who was inviting students to come to his birthday and showed his father his list of invites. Seeing a ninth grader on the list, the dad exclaimed, "You're inviting a ninth grader to your birthday?!? Back when my*

HYDE

Discovery Process

[MODULE]

CLEAR THE DECKS

[LESSON]

Stop-Start-Continue

Overview & Purpose

It is one thing to commit to developing inner leadership and strive for a unique potential; it is another to have a method that can help us determine whether we are, in fact, doing so. Stop-Start-Continue is an exercise that can help keep us on track. This exercise can be done with almost any group or family endeavor.

Social-Emotional Learning Connection

▸ Social Awareness: The abilities to understand the perspectives of and empathize with others, including those from diverse backgrounds, cultures, and contexts.

  ▸ Showing concern for the feelings of others

  ▸ Identifying diverse social norms, including unjust ones

  ▸ Recognizing situational demands and opportunities

▸ Relationship Skills: The abilities to establish and maintain healthy and supportive relationships and to effectively navigate settings with diverse individuals and groups.

  ▸ Practicing teamwork and collaborative problem-solving

  ▸ Showing leadership in groups

▸ Responsible Decision Making: The abilities to make caring and constructive choices about personal behavior and social interactions across diverse situations.

  ▸ Anticipating and evaluating the consequences of one's actions

  ▸ Reflecting on one's role to promote personal, family, and community well-being

  ▸ Evaluating personal, interpersonal, community, and institutional impacts

Figure 5.1   Hyde Discovery Process Lesson (Stop-Start-Continue)
Malcolm Gauld & Hyde Institute

Stop-Start-Continue (cont.)

Learning Objectives

► Students will identify actions and behaviors their Discovery Group can *start* engaging in to improve group dynamics and achieve better outcomes.

► Students will identify actions and behaviors their Discovery Group can *stop* engaging in to improve group dynamics and achieve better outcomes.

► Students will identify actions and behaviors their Discovery Group should *continue* engaging in to improve group dynamics and achieve better outcomes.

► Students will develop and implement plans to start/stop/ continue actions and behaviors to improve group dynamics and achieve better outcomes.

Materials Needed

☐ No materials are needed for this lesson.

Activity

First, ask students, "What do we have to *stop* doing as a group/ family/school in order to

► show more concern for others,

► exhibit better sportsmanship as a community,

► keep our space clean, and so on.

Next, open the floor for discussion and write students' responses on a board for all to see.

After 10+ minutes ask, "What are the things we need to *start* doing in order to _____?"

Then ask students, "What are the things we need to *stop* doing?"

Finally, ask students, "What are the positive things that we are already doing that we need to *continue* doing?"

[2]

Figure 5.1 Hyde Discovery Process Lesson (Stop-Start-Continue) *(continued)*
Malcolm Gauld & Hyde Institute

Stop-Start-Continue (cont.)

Activity (cont.)

Record students' responses to all three questions. You may choose to have students prioritize the responses after they are displayed on the board.

As a follow-up, you may choose to hold a discussion a week or two later in order to assess progress. The Stop-Start-Continue discussion has been proven to be a great way to improve any group's dynamic and/or effectiveness.

Reflection/ Closing

What did we get out of this lesson?

* *What do we want to accomplish as a group/family/ school/community?*

* *What do we need to stop doing in order to do that?*

* *What do we need to start doing?*

* *What do we need to continue doing?*

* *When should we check back in to assess progress?*

Figure 5.1   Hyde Discovery Process Lesson (Stop-Start-Continue) *(continued)*
Malcolm Gauld & Hyde Institute

Discovery Process

[MODULE]

TRUTH IS MY PRIMARY GUIDE

[LESSON]

The 7-11 Dilemma—What Would You Do?

Overview & Purpose	This exercise offers the idea that a clear conscience offers the best path to a truthful life. It will encourage students to explore the relationship between honesty and concern and help students realize that character (or lack thereof) is expressed as a reflex in real time, often on-the-fly. It will also encourage students to observe and assess their own character reflexes.
Social-Emotional Learning Connection	▶ Self-Awareness: The abilities to understand one's own emotions, thoughts, and values and how they influence behavior across contexts. ▶ Demonstrating honesty and integrity ▶ Responsible Decision-Making: The abilities to make caring and constructive choices about personal behavior and social interactions across diverse situations. ▶ Identifying solutions for personal and social problems ▶ Learning to make a reasoned judgment after analyzing information, data, facts ▶ Anticipating and evaluating the consequences of one's actions
Learning Objective	▶ Students will examine the popular notion of character as "what we do when no one is watching" by analyzing, and describing how they would respond to, various dilemmas.
Materials Needed	☐ Reading: The 7-11 Dilemma
Activity	▶ The teacher reads "The 7-11 Dilemma" to the class and facilitates a discussion.

[1]
© 2021 Hyde School

Figure 5.2 Hyde Discovery Process Lesson (The 7-11 Dilemma)
Malcolm Gauld & Hyde Institute

The 7-11 Dilemma—What Would You Do? (cont.)

**Reflection/
Closing**

What did we get out of this lesson?

First, ask the students, "What would you do?" and listen to a few of their responses.

Then, add a new dynamic to the dilemma:

> "Now let me add a new piece to our story: Imagine that the store clerk, a young woman not much older than you, will be fined for the amount she mistakenly gave you. In other words, the difference will come out of her paycheck."

Ask students:

+ *Does this change your thinking in any way?*

+ *Do you think there is a right thing to do in this situation? Why or why not?*

+ *If you were a parent, is there a way you might hope your children might act in this circumstance?*

Note: Sometimes this exercise triggers a longer than expected discussion. It is not unusual to devote two successive sessions to it. Furthermore, 24 hours in between discussions can add value to the exercise.

Figure 5.2   Hyde Discovery Process Lesson (The 7-11 Dilemma) *(continued)*
Malcolm Gauld & Hyde Institute

The 7-11 Dilemma—What Would You Do?

[READING]

THE 7-11 DILEMMA

The "7-11 Dilemma" has been a Discovery Process staple for decades and has been presented to hundreds of students, teachers, and parents. First, the facts:

You drop in to a 7-11 (convenience store) to grab a quick snack. After settling on a soda and a bag of chips, you head for the cash register. As the third customer in line, you notice that the attendant behind the register is a bit flustered by all the activity in the store. She looks as if she's already had a long day. She is trying to keep her eye on two young teens in the back of the store that she suspects are trying to steal some beef jerky. The customer in front of you is rudely interrupting the transaction in front of him by briskly inquiring about the directions to the local shopping mall, and outside another customer is angrily waving the gasoline pump nozzle because he can't get it to pump any gasoline.

Then it's your turn. The attendant tabulates your purchases. Your purchase totals $2.00, and you give her a ten-dollar bill. Amid the confusion, the attendant takes your ten and says, "OK, that's two dollars. Here's your eight and here's your ten. Next customer!"

Due to her divided attention, the attendant has made your visit to the 7-11 a very profitable one. You walked in with $10, and you are leaving with a soda, a bag of chips, and $18. Furthermore, she is now dealing with the two teens, relieved that they have decided to pay for the beef jerky. It is clear to you that she is oblivious to her blunder.

[3]

Figure 5.2   Hyde Discovery Process Lesson (The 7-11 Dilemma) *(continued)*
Malcolm Gauld & Hyde Institute

HYDE

Discovery Process

FIVE WORDS AND FIVE PRINCIPLES

[L E S S O N]

Aristotle's Golden Mean

Overview & Purpose	The purpose of this lesson is to provide students with an opportunity to take a deeper look at the meaning of the Five Words and Five Principles while exploring how they might apply them to their daily lives.
Social-Emotional Learning Connection	▸ Self-Awareness: The abilities to understand one's own emotions, thoughts, and values and how they influence behavior across contexts. 　▸ Identifying personal, cultural, and linguistic assets 　▸ Identifying one's emotions ▸ Social Awareness: The abilities to understand the perspectives of and empathize with others, including those from diverse backgrounds, cultures, and contexts. 　▸ Taking others' perspectives 　▸ Recognizing strengths in others
Learning Objectives	▸ Students will explain the concept of Aristotle's Golden Mean as a way to describe moral behavior. ▸ Students will explain how the Five Words and Five Principles taken to the extremes or either deficient or excessive can be counterproductive. ▸ Students will analyze how they exhibit the Words and Principles in terms of deficiency versus excessiveness.
Materials Needed	☐ A whiteboard and markers ☐ Aristotle's Golden Mean Grid (optional)

Figure 5.3   Hyde Discovery Process Lesson (Aristotle's Golden Mean)
Malcolm Gauld & Hyde Institute

Aristotle's Golden Mean (cont.)

Activity

You might begin with some rhetorical questions: We all know someone who is dishonest. Is it possible to be *too* honest? How about when being truthful gets to the point of cruelty?

Can one be: Too courageous? Too curious?

Explain that Aristotle perceived moral behavior as the mean between two extremes, with deficiency at one end and excess at the other. (You might then ask: What does deficient mean? How about excessive?)

Then say, "Using Aristotle's model, let's take a look at Courage, the first of the Five Words in the Discovery Process common language. Courage might be represented as cowardice in the deficient extreme and foolhardiness or recklessness in the excess extreme."

Once students understand the model relative to Courage, ask the class to suggest words for both the deficient and excessive extremes for the remaining nine Words/Principles. Near the end of the lesson, you might show them the attached grid as a point of further discussion.

The point of the lesson is that morality is not a black-and-white matter. You might also discuss how another lesson in this module, Truth over Harmony, is purposely NOT stated as Truth instead of Harmony. The distinction might be subtle, but it is an important one.

[2]

Figure 5.3 Hyde Discovery Process Lesson (Aristotle's Golden Mean) *(continued)*
Malcolm Gauld & Hyde Institute

Aristotle's Golden Mean (cont.)

**Reflection/
Closing**

What did we get out of this lesson?

♦ *When you consider your relationship with the Five Words and Five Principles, do you tend toward the deficient side of some?*

♦ *Are there any where you tend toward the excessive side?*

♦ *Can you think of any ways you might look at the Five Words and Five Principles differently than you might have before learning about Aristotle's Golden Mean?*

♦ *Who was Aristotle? Why is he studied by individuals today?*

Figure 5.3　Hyde Discovery Process Lesson (Aristotle's Golden Mean) *(continued)*
Malcolm Gauld & Hyde Institute

friends and I were seniors, we would never have invited any ninth grader to any
of our parties." To which the son responded, "Dad, he's in my Discovery Group.
He's one of my friends. Of course I'm gonna invite him to my birthday party."

Current Halifax superintendent Dr. David Hatfield speaks to the value that
families place on the benefits derived from Discovery Groups: "When we
have families move into our school district and after parents get to know the
Discovery Process, they don't understand why school districts across the state
aren't doing what we're doing."

Furthermore, with pride, Bob and Dave have told me of lifelong friendships, and even marriages, that had their roots in the relationships forged in
middle and high school Discovery Groups.

Perhaps another way to make the point here is that the Halifax and Upper
Dauphin schools that "wowed" me so strongly during my initial visits in 2018
did not have access to the 134 lessons we have since collected and written and
placed in the Discovery Process learning platform. While variations of some
of them had been utilized in both school systems, they had not yet been written, edited, and organized for access at the click of a button as they are now.

We have had a few schools (that had not made a commitment to the
Discovery Group concept) administer some of the lessons to their students.
They did not find them to be substantively effective, and we were not sur-
prised. However, the two entities—the Discovery Groups and the program
lessons—working in tandem can truly serve as a dynamic duo for any school.

At the end of the day, neither the Discovery Process nor any other SEL or
character education program can have significant impact on school cultures
without an all-in commitment. As Amy Chapman and Lisa Miller point out in
their *International Journal of Educational Research* journal article:

> *Many schools have been attempting to address the deficiency in intercon-*
> *nectedness by teaching students to develop personal traits through social and*
> *emotional learning (SEL) programs. However, SEL programs are taught in the*
> *way that other knowledge and skills are taught: building up knowledge and*
> *skills with the hope that students will remember and employ them. Even lead-*
> *ers of SEL note that when these skills are taught "piecemeal," they have little*
> *hope of having any effect, which has led to calls from within SEL to deepen*
> *their work. Thus, a successful approach towards cultivating interconnectedness*
> *and the need to work towards the common good in education must go beyond a*
> *stand-alone program or curriculum. We argue here that the proper approach is*
> *to deliberately design school culture to support each child's innate spirituality.*[1]

With any SEL program, it's all about commitment.

NOTE

1. Chapman, Amy, and Lisa Miller, "Awakened Schools: The Burning Imperative of Pedagogical Relational Culture," *International Journal of Educational Research* 116 (2022): 102089.

Chapter 6

FAQs

Since we began this work, there has been no shortage of frequently asked questions from interested individuals. While nobody wants a long answer these days, trying to understand or explain these questions is a bit like sipping from a firehose. What follows is a response to twenty of the most commonly asked questions, one 200-word (or less) "sip" at a time.

Here is a top-20 list:

1. How does the Discovery Process impact the student culture?
2. Is the Discovery Process an anti-bullying program?
3. Is the Discovery Process a character ed or a social and emotional learning (SEL) program?
4. Is it required for Discovery Groups to be mixed age?
5. What happens during the Daily Check-In?
6. Is the Daily Check-In really necessary?
7. What's the expected time commitment in the schedule?
8. How does this work? What structures need to be in place?
9. Is there a sequence? Does everyone teach the same lesson? Are the lessons repeated?
10. I heard someone say, "It's a culture, not a program." What does that mean?
11. I hear that there's also a student jobs component? What's up with that?
12. Is the Discovery Process a diversity, equity, and inclusion (DEI) program?
13. You claim that the Discovery Process also has a positive personal impact on the teachers. How so?
14. Doesn't all this stuff take away from academic time and detract from performance?
15. I trained to teach math, not supervise all this touchy-feely stuff.
16. What are these "core activities" I have been hearing about?
17. Why SEL?
18. Why choose the Discovery Process over other SEL programs?

19. What about assessment methods?
20. What training and materials does each school receive?

1. How does the Discovery Process impact the student culture?

Participating and fully engaged schools consistently experience five outcomes:

- Students feel safe and cared for and have a sense of connection to school and one another.
- They have better coping skills in day-to-day interactions with both peers and adults.
- The Discovery Process encourages synergistic rapport between younger and older students (younger students look up to older students rather than fear them; older students act as role models for younger students).
- The program leads to advancements in learning due to positive learning attitudes and sharper concentration.
- Teachers feel enriched while experiencing personal growth alongside their students.

2. Is the Discovery Process an anti-bullying program?

No and yes. On the one hand, you won't find any lessons specifically targeting bullying. On the other, when kids are striving to be their best selves and helping each other do the same, you won't have much bullying. As mentioned earlier, one participating principal said, "We used to have a lot of fights here. Today we don't even talk about bullying. It just doesn't happen here anymore."

3. Is the Discovery Process a character education or an SEL program?

Our work with the Discovery Process predates the advent of SEL programs. Still, all 134 lessons in the program are aligned with the Collaborative for Academic, Social, and Emotional Learning standards. And just as importantly, a core belief of all of us at the Hyde Institute is that if you put character first, academic growth and performance will follow.

4. Is it required for Discovery Groups to be mixed age?

No, but it's highly recommended. Participating middle and high schools with mixed-age groups invariably find their younger students look up to (rather than fear) the older kids, and the older kids start acting like big brother/sister role models to the younger ones. The leaders of these schools believe strongly in the mixed-aged approach as the heartbeat of the Discovery Process. The ultimate payoff can be seen in an *esprit de corps* embodied in kids of all ages mixing naturally, respectfully, and with inspiring synergy. That's the stuff of awesome culture!

5. What happens during the Daily Check-In?

The Daily Check-In is a group discussion with the following typical agenda items:

- Setting goals for the day
- Reviewing how yesterday's goals were addressed or met
- Discussing one of the Five Words or Principles
- Completing a debriefing activity or discussing issues at school
- Discussing national issues or current events
- Using "sShout-outs" to praise students for stand-out efforts

We find those minutes set aside at the start of the day for the check-in plant a positive mood in the heads of both kids and teachers, making for a more productive academic day.

6. Is the Daily Check-In really necessary?

Schools leaders invariably cite two crucial benefits resulting from the Daily Check-In. First, 15 minutes at the beginning of the day fuels a positive mood that makes for a far more productive academic day. Second, as one superintendent said, "Sad to say, but for too many of my students, those 15 minutes are the sanest, safest 15 minutes they will experience all day. Every student heads off to class knowing that a close group of peers and teachers truly cares about them."

7. What's the expected time commitment in the schedule?

Thus far, the highest time commitment of any participating school is 15 minutes each morning and one 35-minute activity period per day for a total of 300 minutes per week (50 minutes per day). The lowest commitment is 15 minutes per morning and one period per week for a total of 110 minutes per week. While we strongly recommend the former, we prefer not to contract with a school that does not at least commit to the latter as a minimum.

8. How does this work? What structures need to be in place?

Here's a top-10 list of primary steps from contract to implementation:

1. Download the email addresses of participating teachers into the learning management system and invite the teachers to select a password and log on.
2. Training (live or virtual) program for school leaders designed with the Hyde Institute team.
3. Training program for participating teachers designed with the Hyde Institute team.
4. Organize school homerooms into "Discovery Groups" (mixed-age groups are recommended) consisting of 14–16 students and one or two teachers.
5. Begin each school day with a 15-minute morning "check-in" (see the Daily Check-In module).
6. Engage in at least one of the module lessons (30–45 minutes) per week, preferably one per day.
7. Integrate core activities (gym class, intramurals, community service) into the lessons, with debrief sessions after each.
8. Administer mid-year school climate and culture surveys with assistance from the Hyde Institute.
9. Access daily online chat option with Hyde Institute consultants for service and support.
10. Access monthly instructional webinars presented by the Hyde Institute.

9. Is there a sequence? Does everyone teach the same lesson? Are the lessons repeated?

On the one hand, the Discovery Process offers unlimited flexibility. Typically, the designated leader of the program (e.g., the principal or SEL director) will select a module for the week and either assign a particular lesson or invite teachers to choose one they feel is best suited to their particular group of students. (Note: The lessons are presented in order of complexity and difficulty.)

There is no prescribed formal sequence, and whatever sequence is selected by the school's leadership will undoubtedly be influenced by issues faced and traditions valued by specific schools.

On the other hand, modules 1–10 can help teachers and school leaders internalize the most basic concepts and practices of the program. These include Daily Check-In, the Debrief, Clear the Decks, and Action-Reflection Cycle. Some of these lessons will be "one-and-done" affairs, but some will be presented multiple times. For example, some participating schools will facilitate a simple debrief multiple times per day, for example: after intramurals, at the end of a class, following a school assembly. Similarly, the "Stop-Start-Continue" lesson in the Clear the Decks module serves as a regular "go-to" Daily Check-In or Debrief ice-breaker for many Discovery Process teachers.

10. I heard someone say, "It's a culture, not a program." What does that mean?

OK, it is a program, but the spirit of the effort must guide the specifics of the details. For example, the Caring module in the Discovery Process contains six lessons. It's one thing to conduct one or more of these lessons. It's another thing to point out caring actions—such as Jimmy holding the door for a janitor carrying a mop and pail, or Sally comforting a classmate who is feeling down—as they happen in real time. The Discovery Process is "culture by design." It must begin at the top and be shepherded daily by committed teachers and staff. As powerful as the 134 lessons are, the Discovery Group is the "engine room" of it all.

11. I hear that there's also a student jobs component? What's up with that?

Yes. Pushback on this idea has been surprising to us. How did we arrive at a place where the idea of students helping to maintain the cleanliness of their own learning environment is a radical idea? Schools that do this part of the program typically have students spend 30 minutes once or twice monthly picking up trash, sweeping floors, washing windows, or rearranging classrooms. They also find that they have very little litter (or graffiti!) on school grounds.

12. Is the Discovery Process a DEI program?

We committed to building this program before we had ever heard of DEI. Although this program is not a DEI program per se, its core principles and practices amplify the overall aims of any DEI program.

13. You claim the Discovery Process also has a positive personal impact on the teachers. How so?

When we model the notion that we are all "works in progress," not only do we inspire our students to strive to be the best versions of themselves, we also become better versions of ourselves. Our own sense of purpose can be reignited. Post-COVID, study after study concludes that we (the adults) have never needed this more.

14. Doesn't all this stuff take away from academic time and detract from performance?

It is true that if the students were not doing the 15-minute Check-In every morning or spending 35 minutes at the end of the school day on Discovery Process activities, those 50 minutes could be added to academic studies. (Note: That total of 50 minutes is the most daily time that any school devotes to the Discovery Process.)

Discovery Process administrators and teachers uniformly report increases in test scores and an enhanced seriousness of purpose in the classroom. One assistant principal told us, "Since we adopted this program, fewer misbehaving students have been sent my way. I think that's because the Discovery Process inspires a positive ethic of mutual respect between the students and their teachers." Discovery Process educators invariably find that time set aside for the Discovery Groups serves to "sharpen the saw" of our physical, spiritual, mental, and social/emotional dimensions. And when you get right down to it, isn't that the purpose of SEL?

Speaking personally, one thing I have learned as an educator over the past 45 years: the most important ingredient for academic learning is a positive learning attitude on the part of both the student and the teacher. A few moments devoted to that goal on the front end can result in years of exponential progress on the back end.

15. I trained to teach math, not supervise all this touchy-feely stuff.

The Discovery Process demands as much from the teacher as it demands from the student. That is as it should be with any educational initiative. However, it is neither the teacher's job nor expectation to act as an amateur psychologist. Nearly every state in the United States has mandated SEL as a required part of the educational process.

A generation or two ago, it was fully acceptable for a student to limit their efforts to the clear objective of completing a prescribed menu of academic courses. Today, that narrow set of expectations is no longer deemed sufficient for the student seeking a high school diploma. Why should it be any different for the teacher?

The transition to SEL has placed a higher burden on the teacher—especially veteran teachers—than the student. Whereas most of today's students have come of age with SEL already established in their schools, many veteran teachers have had to retool their skill sets. However, given the deeply troubling rise of cyber-bullying and emotional stresses resulting from the explosion of social media options, the accompanying growth of SEL could not be coming at a better time. In fact, given today's social media environment and the aftereffects of the COVID-19 pandemic, the cost of not reaching out to our students in newly important ways that our predecessors might not have is simply too high.

16. What are these "core activities" I have been hearing about?

This aspect of the program integrates the extracurricular aspect of any school into the mix. A popular slogan of the Discovery Process states, "everybody does everything." We give everything a try. Examples include:

- Intramurals and Team-Building—Sometimes coordinated with a school's physical education program
- Performing Arts—Skits and singing; some schools develop a show
- School-Wide Jobs—Pick up litter, sweep floors, wash windows
- Community Service—Organize a community betterment project

As the program develops, it is common to see the school sports star helping the less athletically inclined student during intramurals and those roles reversed when the students are tackling homework in a challenging course. Not only does everybody do everything, but everybody also helps each other.

17. Why SEL?

Approaching their teens, kids inevitably face a conflict between what is right and what is cool. The best way to help them negotiate this conflict is to ensure a strong school culture. However, one need not look hard for data demonstrating our national problem regarding school culture. To repeat statistics presented earlier:

- As of 2020, all 50 states have passed and enacted anti-bullying legislation.
- The National Center for Education Statistics shows that one in five public school students report being bullied. (Incidents among girls approach one in four.)
- The Centers for Disease Control and Prevention report that over 30 percent of all middle school students have experienced cyber-bullying.

- A 2017 GLSEN National School Climate Survey shows that 60 percent of America's LGBTQ students feel unsafe in school due to their sexual orientation.

Schools simply cannot provide transformative experiences when students spend any time feeling physically threatened, publicly humiliated, or virtually maligned. (Note: That same National Center for Education Statistics report indicates that 41 percent of those who have been bullied live in fear of it happening again.) At the same time, it is not enough for a school to be a place where kids feel safe. School must be a place where they feel encouraged, indeed inspired, to test their abilities, hopes, and dreams.

18. Why choose the Discovery Process over other SEL programs?

It's all about inspiration. Safety alone is a good enough reason to offer SEL in our schools. However, safety, as a goal unto itself, is also a pretty low bar. Inspiring school cultures demand the absence of some elements and the presence of others. Bullying, prejudice, cheating, and indifference must be absent. Respect, creativity, effort, and inclusiveness must be present.

Even if a school manages to make bullying absent, it does not necessarily follow that an uplifting *esprit de corps* will be present. Reflecting the mathematician's maxim of "necessary but not sufficient," contemporary anti-bullying programs tend to fall into a "make it absent" default zone, one heavy on identifying and penalizing behavioral violations. Hence, it is perhaps not surprising that conventional SEL state standards are commonly heavy on compliance, obedience, and cooperation and light on ambition, chutzpah, and pursuit of dreams. Rather than start with what to do about bullying, the Hyde Discovery Process asks (and answers) the more holistic question: What to do about inspiration?

19. What about assessment methods?

Perhaps the most important part of a school culture is how kids and teachers feel about it and how hard they are willing to work to uphold it. Hence, we seek a standard of 80 percent approval (i.e., *Feel Very Good* or *Good*) regarding the following indicators of our surveys at the conclusion of each year:

- Physical and emotional safety
- Freedom of expression ("I feel encouraged by my peers to try new things")
- Awareness of and respect for DEI

- Personal accomplishment
- My peers/teachers know me and help me do my best.

To measure these outcomes, the Hyde Institute has been working with the Excellence with Integrity Institute (www.ewii.org) to develop an evaluative school culture survey for all students, teachers, and parents to be distributed in the fall and spring of each year. Nationally respected for its work with schools on culture, Excellence with Integrity Institute's surveys intentionally focus on three essential components of caring communities: Kids feel . . . 1. known and needed, 2. safe and cared for, and 3. that they have a role in shaping their environment.

20. What training and materials does each school receive?

The product suite received by the client schools contain five components:

- 25 modules housing 134 lessons (all aligned with the Collaborative for Academic, Social, and Emotional Learning standards) and instructional videos, which are all accessible to teachers in a password-protected online portal
- Each portal is personalized to each participating school (e.g., it includes school colors, photos, slogans, mottos, etc.)
- Separate training programs for teachers and school leaders
- Separate online handbooks for teachers, school leaders, and facilitators
- One (per teacher) hardcopy Teacher Performance Workbook
- School culture assessment tool distributed, tabulated, and analyzed by an independent third party
- Monthly training webinars
- Membership in an online community for the sharing of best practices

Getting Started

So, your school is about to embark on the Discovery Process. Does your first look at the learning management system portal have you feeling like you're sipping from a firehose? You're asking, *Where do we even begin? How about a roadmap for some initial moves?*

Here are ten pieces of advice assembled after discussions with some of the early adopters of the Discovery Process.

1. Commit to the mixed-age Discovery Groups. This idea may represent a substantive change from the way you have previously done things, but

the mixed-aged format invariably brings positive change in how students interact with each other. Once the students buy in to this idea, schools find that the younger students look up to (rather than fear) the older ones who, in turn, start acting like big brother/sister role models. They also tend to find that exclusionary social cliques start to fade from prominence on the school social scene.

As for how to organize such groups, there are many options, including any number of randomizing software programs. A section of the training program specifically designed for school leaders addresses this structure.

Consider keeping your Discovery Groups together throughout the students' time at the school. Both the Halifax and Upper Dauphin (Pennsylvania) schools keep their groups together year after year in order to ensure continuity of relationships.

2. Commit to the Daily Check-In. Again, this might represent a substantive change for your school, but those schools who have done this for a period would never go back to not doing it. It fosters caring, support, and togetherness. It also makes for a better school day thanks to curious and respectful learners and fewer students needing to be sent to the assistant principal's office for disciplinary reasons.
3. Discuss and plan your training needs with the Hyde Institute team. While the full training program is a 3-hour session for the school leader and two 3.5-hour sessions for the faculty, every school we have worked with has done it differently. Flexibility is a hallmark of both the program and its training.
4. Encourage your teachers to log on to the learning management system platform and surf around a bit. You should, too! Familiarize yourselves with the training components, especially the three virtual handbooks designed for specific audiences: Teachers, Leaders, and Facilitators. Leaf through the Teacher's Performance Workbook (the only hard copy piece in the whole program).
5. Remember: Teachers are participants who model the process as much as facilitate it. Sure, you're in charge, but few things are more powerful for kids to see than adults acting like works in progress.
6. Schedule a minimum of one period per week where students and teachers engage together in one of the Discovery Process lessons. (Note: We recommend one period per day.)
7. Seek out and capitalize on the teachable moment. It's one thing to facilitate a lesson on caring or concern for others. It's another to take notice and give a shout-out to the student holding the door open for a janitor

who is pulling a bucket and mop into the hallway. Whenever you see kids acting in a manner that reflects the principles espoused by your school, stop and make a big deal about it!

8. Don't avoid the jobs component. Even if it's only once or twice a month, students who spend some time maintaining the cleanliness of their learning environment are far less likely to litter the grounds or spray graffiti on the walls. It won't be popular in the beginning, but it will become a source of pride over time.

9. Debrief, debrief, and debrief some more. While the Debrief module covers the process in detail, it all boils down to someone asking, "OK. How did we just do?" You will know that the Discovery Process has begun to be integrated into your school when you start seeing the soccer coach doing it after a challenging game or even a practice, the performing arts teacher doing it after a rehearsal, or a teacher doing it after intramurals. You'll *really* know it has taken hold when the kids start doing it without you.

10. "Everybody does everything." Adopt that ethos. Sports and performing arts are not just for the kids who are already good at them. We all give it a try. Watch cliques vanish from the scene as the students collectively realize that it is not uncool to try something and maybe look bad.

BONUS: Be patient. Avoid assessing the program's value while you're doing it. Instead, pick a date off in the future when you will discuss how it's all going.

Conscience-Driven Graduates with Character Reflexes

Returning to Aristotle and habits, it is important to remember that character happens in real time. We may allot 30–45 minutes to an academic period devoted to a Discovery Process lesson, but life tends to demand split-second decisions from us. That fact leads to a clear conclusion: What we character educators really want to do is develop character reflexes in the service of conscience.

Character Reflexes

Most seasoned teachers cultivate some go-to shticks they resort to on a regular basis. One of mine is an annual school assembly where I begin by passing a soccer ball back and forth with random students in the audience. As expected, each student catches the ball and then tosses it back to me. The mood in the room reflects a mix of humor and puzzlement.

After maybe a minute of this back and forth, I set the ball down and tell a story about a professional European soccer coach who years ago ran a pre-season clinic for our players. During his first session, he did the very same thing with the soccer ball, and the students responded as these students did. He then observed, "If I did this in Europe, the kids would never reach up with their hands. Instead, they would head the ball, trap the ball on their knees, or juggle it with their feet. Until American kids get to the point where their first impulse is not to reach up with their hands, the Americans will never be competitive in World Cup soccer."

As soon as he finished his comment, a light bulb went off in my head: We want to graduate young men and women who will have excellent character reflexes. They will be truthful, act with courage, step up to lead, exhibit enterprising curiosity, care for others—and do all of the above without thinking about it.

Ironically, these split-second reflexes require lifelong maintenance. During my meeting with our students, I also tell the story of how I once sat in a New York subway car heading out to visit a Bronx public school. Deep in thought about some pressing issue I now cannot recall, I was oblivious to the pregnant woman, holding a baby in one arm and a handbag in the other, standing nearby. A moment later, another passenger got out of his seat and gave it to this woman. I was embarrassed and more than a little ashamed of myself to realize that my concern reflexes had failed me. They needed some work.

Hence, one doesn't just learn this character stuff once and then move on to the next lesson. As an analogy, imagine a basketball coach on the final practice before a big game against a team known to have a killer full-court press. Here's what that coach would not say: "Well, team, remember last month when we spent part of a practice on techniques for breaking a full-court press. Review your notes on that and we will be all set for tomorrow."

No way! That coach would have the second team act as the pressing team and the first team would be drilled, drilled, and drilled some more until they mastered the techniques and teamwork necessary for breaking that press. The coach would continue the drilling until the press-breaking had become second nature. Sometimes the character educator must act like that coach.

Character demands a lifelong commitment, one that requires ongoing renewal and maintenance. It's one thing to think about the right thing to do in a given situation. It's quite another to do it "on the fly." That's our goal.

Conscience-Driven People

Harvard psychologist Lawrence Kohlberg's (1927–1987) exhaustive research suggested that people are not simply moral or immoral, but that there are degrees of morality. He identified three stages with two levels within each. At risk of oversimplification, the three stages are as follows.

Stage One people are concerned solely with the direct consequences of their actions. The decision to obey or disobey is based primarily on punishment and reward.

Stage Two reflects social norms. Speaking of subways, Washington subway riders may seem less likely to litter than their New York counterparts. The point: both groups seem to reflect their corresponding norms. Stage Two is a higher level of morality than Stage One, but it is still based on reactions to others rather than conscience.

Stage Three embodies a conscience-driven life. Stage Three people ask, "What is right?" And then they try to live their lives in accordance with that perception of right.

Our Mission

The Discovery Process exists to help any school design, implement, evaluate, and continuously improve its culture. It is built upon the belief that character is what matters most in both bad and good times. The Hyde Institute seeks to create and nurture a national network of participating schools.

The guiding premise of the Discovery Process is captured in a single sentence: *Every individual is gifted with a unique potential that defines a destiny.* This premise has its roots in the 1966 founding of Hyde School, a Maine character-based boarding school. Hyde public school models have since been established in a number of US cities.

Beginning in the late 1990s, a cohort of rural Pennsylvania public schools began redesigning their schools in accordance with this premise and the Hyde philosophy. In 2019, leaders from Hyde and these Pennsylvania school systems joined forces with the goal of combining the best of the Hyde and Pennsylvania models to scale the results to a national audience. In 2022, the initial cohort of beta schools began implementing the program.

PART 3

Character

Chapter 7

So, What Is Character?

Throughout this book, several references have been made to character: "character education" and "character-based" teaching, parenting, programming, etc. I have even described my career as having been spent in the "character ed lane." Some readers may be wondering, *What does that even mean? How do you define character?*

While those are fair questions deserving an answer, attempts at defining character can be fraught with peril. They can be polarizing. They can be too vague. They can even be too specific. (See next paragraph.) Any attempt can trigger enough debate to cause the erstwhile "definer" to settle for Supreme Court Justice Potter Stewart's famous definition of pornography: "I know it when I see it." (On the one hand, it's more than a bit weird to ponder the idea that a single definition could be utilized interchangeably to define the words "pornography" and "character." On the other, that odd coincidence supports the point of "character" being a very hard word to define.)

There are a number of popular definitions I like but resist using because they don't tell the whole story. For example, consider one that is popular among educators and parents, including those at Discovery Process schools: "Character is what you do when no one is watching."

On the one hand, it can be that. However, that definition also falls into the mathematician's maxim of "necessary but not sufficient." After all, some of the most dramatic expressions of character the world has seen have occurred when seemingly everyone, or at least, a very big crowd, was watching:

- The "Miracle on Ice" when the 1980 US Olympic hockey team beat both the odds and the Russians at Lake Placid
- The Hoyts—the father-and-son team that competed in countless Ironman triathlons with Dick (dad) pushing Rick, his son with cerebral palsy, in a wheelchair
- Dr. Martin Luther King orating to the world from the steps of the Lincoln Memorial

- Teen environmentalist Greta Thunberg's all-in commitment to saving the planet

And why did millions across the world tune in during the summer of 2022 to watch Serena Williams' final appearance at the US Open? (It was ESPN's most-watched tennis telecast since the network was founded in 1978.) Sure, people wanted to see good tennis, but that character "thing" was most definitely in the air and people wanted to see and feel it. One thing's for sure about Serena and the other four examples listed before her: It could not be said that no one was watching!

Another popular quote, one often uttered by a colleague who was a legendary high school wrestling coach, states, "Character is being able to say 'No' to yourself." While that sentiment is highly applicable to the endless physical conditioning and the perpetual and ascetic dieting common to wrestlers, character can also mean saying "Yes!" to yourself.

For example, in his book *The Soul's Code*, James Hillman tells this powerful story that takes place one night in New York City in 1933 with Ella Fitzgerald doing amateur night at the Harlem Opera House. She was scheduled to dance, but at the last minute decided to sing and ended up winning first prize!

The young Ella made a split-second decision to say "Yes!" to herself, to her unique potential. (Note: When I have used this story at school community meetings over the years, I conclude the session with a 1960 live recording of Ms. Fitzgerald singing a version of the Bobby Darin hit "Mack the Knife." This version is particularly memorable because she forgets the lyrics but forges ahead with an amazing rendition complete with her signature scat singing and lyrics made up on the spot. If nothing else, she proves beyond all doubt that she was meant to sing![1])

Over the years, I have seen many of my students take charge of their lives by saying "Yes" to themselves:

- The four-time New England Prep School wrestling champion who left college after one month in order to become a stand-up comic. (When he called to tell me of his plans, all I could say in response was, "But, I've never heard you tell a joke!") He went on to perform on the *Tonight Show*, *Late Show with David Letterman*, and *Last Comic Standing*, and does hundreds of dates across the country each year. (Years later, I said to him, "Hey, what do I know?)
- The young woman who played on my soccer team and went on to become an ordained Episcopal minister.

- Another who has established and leads a psychology practice of over a dozen therapists who help individuals and couples of all ages better their lives.
- The fraternal twin brothers who are recognized internationally for having completed several first kayak descents on rivers around the world.
- The many students I have known or worked with who went on to become the first members of their families to attend college.

For sure, these individuals had to muster the discipline necessary to say "No" to themselves in order to develop the skills and acumen necessary for them to pursue their respective paths. However, they also had to say "Yes!" to themselves to take these paths in the first place.

At various points in this book, reference has been made to some of the characterizations of character that have influenced the Discovery Process. For example, Matt Davidson and Thomas Lickona's delineation of performance character and moral character helped close some open loops in our thinking.

Furthermore, Tom's definition of character education as "the deliberate effort to cultivate virtue in its cognitive, emotional, and behavioral dimensions through every phase of school life" may come the closest to describing what character educators try to do. His "every phase of school life" qualifier counters those who may perceive character education as an "add on."

Reference has also been made to Kevin Ryan's notion of "to know, to do, and to love the good." More recently, we have been influenced by Angela Duckworth. Here is a passage from her CharacterLab website:

We define character as everything we do to help other people as well as ourselves. . . . As an organizing principle, we separate character strengths into three dimensions. Strengths of heart, such as gratitude, enable harmonious relationships with other people. Strengths of will, such as grit and self-control, enable achievement. Strengths of mind, such as curiosity, enable independent thinking.

Somewhere along the way, I picked up something that I have seen attributed to both Aristotle (392–322 BC) and Winston Churchill (1874–1965) that describes character as the "habit of making right decisions." While that is also very specific, I like the "habit" qualifier. Habit is key to character. Another Aristotle quote speaks to that: "Moral excellence comes about as a result of habit. We become just by doing just acts, temperate by doing temperate acts, brave by doing brave acts." There's that climate (feel) versus culture (habits) thing again.

There have also been some quotes that may fall short of a full definition, per se, but can help in clarifying understanding. Some of these include the following:

"Character, like a photograph, develops in darkness."

—Yousuf Karsh (1908–2002), photographer

"Be more concerned with your character than your reputation, because your character is what you really are, while your reputation is merely what others think you are."

—John Wooden (1910–2010), basketball coach

Perhaps Wooden was channeling his inner Abraham Lincoln: *"Character is like a tree and reputation like a shadow. The shadow is what we think of it; the tree is the real thing."*

"Parents can only give good advice or put them [their children] on the right paths, but the final forming of a person's character lies in their own hands."

—Anne Frank (1929–1945)

"Talent is best formed in solitude. Character is best formed in the stormy billows of the world."

—Goethe (1749–1832)

"Character cannot be developed in ease and quiet. Only through experience of trial and suffering can the soul be strengthened, ambition inspired, and success achieved."

—Helen Keller

"Just because you are a character does not mean you have character."

—A quote popular with Hyde School students!

Over the years, I have written scores of blog posts, editorials, and various compositions about character. While I make no claim to having ever hit the mark, I sometimes feel as though teachers are like jazz musicians. We riff on various ideas and methodologies in a never-ending effort to connect with our students. Sometimes we find a groove and feel a sense of cognitive synergy between them and ourselves. Then we try to "bookmark" that groove and return to it in future sessions. Sometimes that groove evolves into a riff and we become one with it.

Here are a few riffs that speak to my view of character ed.

Character Cannot Be Taught

First, I subscribe to two premises: "character cannot be taught" and "context matters as much, if not more, than site."

Regarding the first, character is inspired, not imparted. We don't pour character into our students; we summon it forth with values-forming challenges and experiences. In his 1992 book *Dumbing Us Down*, former New York State Teacher of the Year John Gatto presents a comparison of the painter and the sculptor as a metaphor for great teaching.

A painter, he explains, begins with a blank canvas and transforms it by *adding* patterns of color to create a new design. A sculptor begins with a mass of stone and transforms it by *subtracting* matter to reveal a shape that was always there, waiting to be exposed to the world. Gatto maintains that the great teachers are sculptors rather than painters. I agree.

If teaching is your calling—I define calling as two stages beyond "job" and one stage beyond "career"—one would assume that more than a few deeply appreciative parents have approached you at a graduation and said something like, "Thank you so much. You and this school truly *gave* my kid character (*or* motivation *or* inspiration *or* whatever synonym)." At risk of being labeled a Scrooge, I tell my younger colleagues, "Enjoy these well-earned accolades, but don't believe them. After all, they are inaccurate."

We don't *give* our students anything. Instead, we help them uncover something that was always there. It might be blocked by a lack of confidence or a pile of family dysfunction. Great teachers remove the barriers and ignite that confidence to help a kid take off.

Hence, I try to teach according to a simple creed: No kid makes it in life solely because of me, and no kid fails to make it solely because of me. However, more kids will make it if I do my best.

Context and Sites

As for "context" and "sites," imagine a high ropes course, a very powerful character development *site* utilized by many schools today. The high ropes course fosters courage, risk-taking, and trust. However, what happens after Debbie descends from the ropes course, unfastens her harness, unstraps her helmet, and debriefs on the experience with her peers? Let's assume that she goes home to parents who are not striving to develop these qualities of courage, risk-taking, and trust. Let's assume she returns home to a dysfunctional family. Debbie will have considerable difficulty receiving the maximum benefit of the ropes course if she spends most of her time living in a context that either does not reinforce or runs counter to its lessons.

As educators, we are being arrogant, foolish, or both if we believe that the power of our character *site*work will overpower the dynamic of the daily *context* of the lives of our students. Thus, we must nurture that context at every possible opportunity with the same vigor that we currently apply to developing our learning sites.

Think of the benefit to Debbie if her parents were to experience the ropes course *with* her. In addition to the Discovery Process, the Hyde Institute also offers a parenting program called *The Biggest Job* that joins school and family in a character development curriculum.

Our Guardian, Our Catapult

Q: OK, Malcolm, that's all well and good, but you still haven't told us your definition of character. So, what is it?

A: **Character is that inner voice that serves as our guardian against temptation and our catapult to greatness.**

My definition, informed by people, readings, and experiences during my pedagogic journey, perceives character as a dual force that serves as our guardian against temptation and our catapult to greatness. By greatness, I don't mean in comparison to everybody else. I am referring to one's personal best. If it is true that each of us has a date with a unique personal destiny, character development is the vehicle that can take us there. Without it, we're left standing by the side of the road.

While writing this section, I pulled up Google search and typed in "Cartoon characters with a devil on one shoulder and an angel on the other." If you do this and click Search, you will find pages and pages of cartoons featuring this dynamic in cartoon series ranging from *The Flintstones* to *The Simpsons*.

As a kid in Sunday School, with my head bowed, I recall the images of these characters popping up in my head whenever we would get to the "Lead us not into temptation" passage of the Lord's Prayer. To me, it seemed clear that misfortunes would abound and multiply for those who fell victim to the cartoon devil but, at the same time, the rewards of heeding the angel seemed fuzzy to me.

It sometimes seems that kids may look at contemporary character education and social and emotional learning programs in a similar way. It's as though they're thinking, *I see what I get if I mess up at school* . . . (detention, a scolding, the assistant principal telephones the parents, etc.) . . . *but I do not see what I get if I toe the line and exert myself to any degree.* Even though any rational person knows that we need character in good times and bad, in the end, it is very easy for our teaching and our parenting to become ensnared in the guardian trap.

Character education and social and emotional learning programs become long on guardian and short on catapult because they tend to equate "character program" with "solution to a problem" (e.g., bullying). For example, parents and teachers might think, *Hmm . . . Maybe a character program would cut down on bullying on the playground.* Once the problem is "solved," the character program returns to the shelf only to gather dust. It is important to remember that character is like a muscle: You either use it or lose it. It cannot grow on the shelf.

Because we, as a society, often call upon our schools to focus on the urgent at the expense of the important, our schools often find themselves mired in that guardian trap. While the Discovery Process seeks to balance both sides of the guardian/catapult equation, it could be said that it places its 51-percent emphasis on the catapult side in order to fuel an inspiring excitement for the road ahead and causes a number of our contemporary school culture problems to fade in the rearview.

The Discovery Group is the most critical driver of that inspiring culture. As these groups meet and bond over time, their members (both individually and collectively) experience personal growth as they engage in some recurring continuums of human development that we have identified and codified for the benefit of our teachers. One of these is the Charles Reade poem presented earlier in this book:

Sow an act, reap a habit
Sow a habit, reap a character
Sow a character, reap a destiny.

Another continuum is one we call *Motions/Effort/Excellence*. Whether attempting to master a skill or develop a productive attitude, we have observed that kids (and adults) tend to evolve through three phases:

1. The motions of responsible behavior
2. The beginnings of authentic effort and enterprising initiative
3. The commitment to excellence and one's personal best

Hang around a Discovery Process school classroom, athletic team, or performing arts production, and you'll see tangible evidence of all three phases in operation. (See the Best Possible Me/Us module for a lesson on the Motions/Effort/Excellence continuum.) It is also common for students to reflect different phases in different endeavors. For example, the star athlete might reflect excellence in basketball, effort in Spanish, and motions in performing arts or community service.

A third continuum is one we call Rigor/Synergy/Conscience:

1. Rigor: Accepting accountability for your end of things
2. Synergy: No one is an island (1 + 1 = 3); we all offer and accept help
3. Conscience: The search for one's destiny through a commitment to excellence

As a longtime teacher of US history and government, I have been known to sometimes substitute these three stages for our country's three branches of government:

1. Executive Branch = Rigor
2. Legislative Branch = Synergy
3. Judicial Branch = Conscience

I then proceed to puzzle students with questions like: So how are you coming along with your executive function? What is the quality of your legislative alliances these days? Are you judicious in your daily affairs? Are you becoming wiser? How's your sense of justice at this point in your life? Sometimes it makes them think more about these concepts. Sometimes they simply think I'm off my rocker. Such is the teacher's life!

In any case, all three components are important factors in our personal growth and development whether we are students, teachers, or parents.

As seriously as we take our college preparatory function at our school, we have also taken to warning our students, "When all is said and done, you better have something going for you besides a college degree on your resume. That's just not going to do for you in the future what it might have done for your parents in the past."

When I observe the adult lives of my former students, their college affiliation is not the determining factor in their success, fulfillment, or happiness. These elusive qualities have far more to do with attitude than they do with aptitude. They are all about those Five Words and Principles and the common language we espouse.

To remind myself of this, I keep a homemade poster on the wall directly across from my desk (Fig. 7.1). I often say to our faculty and our parents that "the meter starts running at thirty." That's the endgame. A rigorous and carefully planned academic curriculum can assist our efforts to accomplish this endgame. However, prospects for success are vastly improved when we support our students with values-forming challenges that can help them gain a personal confidence that comes from the knowledge that one has:

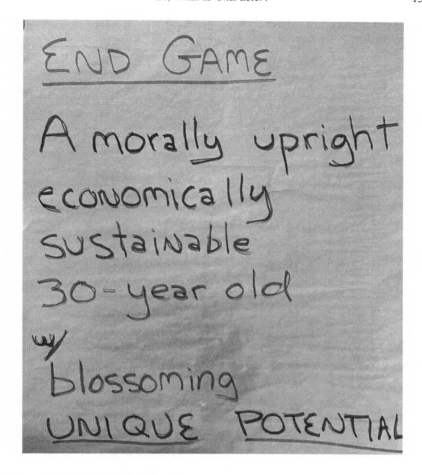

Figure 7.1   Sign in Author's Office
Malcolm Gauld

- been tested socially and emotionally on those qualities espoused in a carefully considered common language;
- tried and failed and tried and succeeded with a range of challenges, sometimes in public view of peers and mentors;
- received personal help from peers and mentors while offering the same;
- tested oneself with both familiar and unfamiliar challenges; and
- learned and grown personally alongside adult role models who care enough to provide both challenge and support.

With that "endgame" in mind, the Discovery Process was created to help schools manifest both guardian and catapult.

At the end of the day, character development is most effective when all the players involved regard themselves as works in progress. An indescribable but unmistakable synergy fills the air when that happens.

Over the years, my wife and I have facilitated *The Biggest Job* parenting workshops with parents across the United States and in Europe and Asia. It has become tradition for us to conclude each of these workshops with an exchange that once took place 50 years ago between a reporter and the great cellist Pablo Casals (1876–1973) during the final year of his life:

> *Reporter:* "Mr. Casals, you have long been considered the greatest cellist in the world. At age ninety-six, why do you still practice six hours a day?"
>
> *Casals:* "Because I think I'm making *progress*."

Schools with strong and inspiring cultures view character development the same way that Pablo Casals viewed playing the cello. It is a lifelong process demanding authentic participation from all concerned.

NOTE

1. Hillman, James, *The Soul's Code: In Search of Character and Calling* (New York: Random House, 1996).

Bibliography

A number of books have found their way into this book and influenced the development of the Discovery Process. A short list would include the following.

Argyris, Chris, and Donald Schon. *Organizational Learning: A Theory of Action Perspective*. Boston: Addison-Wesley, 1978.

Brooks, Kim. *Small Animals: Parenthood in the Age of Fear*. New York: Flatiron Books, 2019.

Collins, Jim. *Built to Last: Successful Habits of Visionary Companies*. New York: Harper Collins, 1994.

Davidson, Matt, and Thomas Lickona. *Smart and Good High Schools: Integrating Excellence and Ethics for Success in School, Work and Beyond*. Cortland, NY: Center for the 4th and 5th R, SUNY Courtland, 2005.

Dewey, John. *Democracy and Education*. Stuttgart: Macmillan, 1916.

Dweck, Carol. *The Growth Mindset: The New Psychology of Success*. New York: Random House, 2006.

Gatto, John. *Dumbing Us Down: The Hidden Curriculum of Compulsory Schooling*. Gabriola, BC, Canada: New Society Publishers, 1992.

Gauld, Laura, and Malcolm Gauld. *The Biggest Job We'll Ever Have*. New York: Scribner, 2002.

Haidt, Jonathan, and Greg Lukianoff. *The Coddling of the American Mind: How Good Intentions and Bad Ideas Are Setting Up a Generation for Failure*. New York: Penguin Books, 2019.

Hillman, James. *The Soul's Code: In Search of Character and Calling*. New York: Random House, 1996.

Miller, Lisa. *The Awakened Brain: The New Science of Spirituality and Our Quest for an Inspired Life*. New York: Random House, 2021.

Rockefeller, Steven C. *Spiritual Democracy and Our Schools: Renewing the American Spirit with Education for the Whole Child*. London: Clearview Publishing, 2022.

Index

About the Author

A second-generation educator, **Malcolm Gauld** has spent most of his adult life as a teacher, athletic coach, and administrator. He served for more than 30 years as head of school and president at Hyde School in Bath, Maine. He serves today as executive director of the Hyde Institute, an organization he established to create and provide character-based learning opportunities to school communities across the country and beyond.

Malcolm and his wife Laura, current president and chief executive officer of Hyde School, co-authored *The Biggest Job We'll Ever Have: The Hyde School Program for Character-Based Education and Parenting* (2002), and have presented parenting workshops to thousands of parents across the United States as well as in Canada, Asia, and Europe. The book was translated into a Mandarin Chinese edition in 2018.

Malcolm is also the author of two *College Success Guaranteed* books (Rowman & Littlefield, 2011 and 2014); one is meant for students, the other for parents.

A graduate of Hyde and Fessenden schools, Malcolm received his bachelor's in history at Bowdoin College and his master's in education at Harvard University. He was honored to study as a Klingenstein Fellow at Teachers College, Columbia University.

A lifelong athlete, he plays basketball and Grand Masters lacrosse, and has completed several marathons. An avid waterman, he has twice competed in Sea Paddle NYC, a stand-up paddle circumnavigation of Manhattan for the cause of autism research. He and Laura are the proud parents of three grown children: Mahalia, Scout, and Harrison.